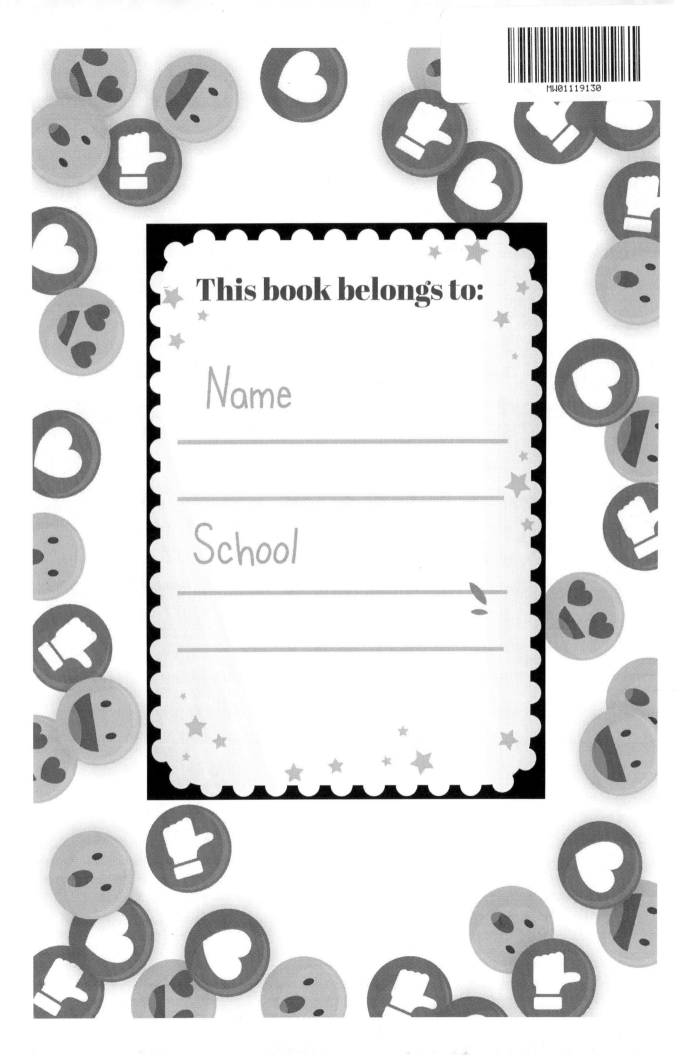

This book belongs to:

Name

School

9th Grade Math:Test Your Knowledge Refresher

1. Addends are numbers_____
   a. used in an addition problem.
   b. used in an addition or multiplication problem.
   c. used in an subtraction problem.

2. What is an example of an Addend?
   a. In 9 + 1 = 10, the 9 and the 10 are addends.
   b. In 8 - 3 = 5, the 8 and the 3 are addends.
   c. In 8 + 3 = 11, the 8 and the 3 are addends.

3. What is a fact family?
   a. a group of math facts or equations created using the same set of numbers.
   b. is when you take one number and add it together a number of times.
   c. is taking away one or more items from a group of items.

4. Which is an example of a fact family?
   a. 2, 4, and 6: 2 x 2 = 4, 4 x 2 = 8, 6 − 2 = 4, and 6 − 4 = 2.
   b. 1, 2, and 12: 1 + 1 = 2, 2 + 2 = 4, 12 − 12 = 0, and 12 − 2 = 10.
   c. 10, 2, and 12: 10 + 2 = 12, 2 + 10 = 12, 12 − 10 = 2, and 12 − 2 = 10.

5. The fact family for 3, 8 and 24 is a set of four multiplication and division facts. Which one is correct?
   a. 3 × 8 = 24| 8 × 3 = 24| 24 ÷ 3 = 8| 24 ÷ 8 = 3
   b. 3 + 8 = 11| 8 × 3 = 24| 8 ÷ 8 = 0| 24 ÷ 8 = 3
   c. 3 × 3 = 9| 8 × 3 = 24| 24 + 3 = 27| 24 ÷ 8 = 3

6. A prime number is_____
   a. the ways that numbers are combined to make new numbers.
   b. any number that is only divisible by itself and 1.
   c. the number you are rounding followed by 5, 6, 7, 8, or 9.

7. Examples of prime numbers_____
   a. 2, 8 and 15
   b. 2, 5 and 17
   c. 4, 6 and 10

8. Numbers such as _____ are not prime, because they are divisible by more than just themselves and 1.
   a. 2 or 7
   b. 5 or 11
   c. 15 or 21

9. Prime factor is the factor_____
   a. of the first number which is NOT a prime number.
   b. of the smallest to greatest prime number starting with 0..
   c. of the given number which is a prime number.

10. The prime factors of 15 _____
    a. are 3 and 5 (because 3×5=15, and 3 and 5 are prime numbers)
    b. are 5 and 10 (because 5+10=15, and 10 and 5 are prime numbers)
    c. are 25 and 10 (because 25-10=15, and 10 and 5 are prime numbers)

11. A factor tree is a _____
    a. natural numbers greater than one that are not products of two smaller natural numbers.
    b. diagram that is used to break down a number into its factors until all the numbers left are prime.
    c. is divisible by 1, and it's divisible by itself.

12. The greatest common denominator is the _____
    a. smallest positive integer that multiplies the numbers without a remainder.
    b. largest negative integer that subtracts the numbers without a remainder.
    c. largest positive integer that divides the numbers without a remainder.

13. The greatest common factor of 8 and 12 is_____?
    a. 12
    b. 6
    c. 4

14. The lowest common denominator is the _____?
    a. lowest common multiple of the denominators of a set of fractions.
    b. lowest common multiple of the denominators of a group of numbers divided by 10.
    c. lowest common subtraction of the first number of a set of fractions.

15. What is the LCD of 12 and 8?
    a. 12 and 8 is 24
    b. 12 and 8 is 32
    c. 12 and 8 is 20

16. This math concept tells you that to divide means to split fairly.
    a. Division
    b. Addition
    c. Algebra

17. Reduce 48/28 to lowest terms.
    a. 12/5
    b. 12/7
    c. 7/28

18. Which of the following fractions CANNOT be reduced further?
    a. 5/3
    b. 33/12
    c. 16/9

19. It is possible to make a fraction simpler without completely simplifying it.
    a. True
    b. False

20. Factor 18 into prime factors:
    a. $18 = 3 * 3 * 2$
    b. $18 = 2 * 3 * 3$
    c. $18 = 1 * 3 * 2$

21. An improper fraction is one where the numerator is smaller than the denominator.
    a. True
    b. False

22. Fractions that have a numerator with a higher value than the denominator
    a. simple fractions
    b. simplified fractions
    c. improper fractions

9th Grade Reading Comprehension: Social Media Safety

Interactions	policies	relationship	post	pop-ups
incidents	identity	connect	Personal	logins
negative	harmful	restrictive	steal	privacy
passwords	viruses	platform	abuse	security

In the last 20 years, socializing has evolved dramatically. _____ between people are referred to as socializing. At one time, socializing meant getting together with family and friends. It now frequently refers to accessing the Internet via social media or websites that allow you to _____ and interact with other people.

One of the first things you can do to protect yourself while online occurs before you even visit a social media website. Ascertain that your computer is outfitted with up-to-date computer _____ software. This software detects and removes _____ that are harmful to your computer. When you use your computer, these viruses can sometimes hack into it and _____ your information, such as _____. Create strong _____ for all of your social media accounts. This is necessary to prevent others from accessing your social media account.

Internet security settings are pre-installed on all computers. These can be as loose or as _____ as you want them to be. To be safe, it is recommended that the Internet security settings be set to medium or higher. This enables your computer to block _____ and warn you when you are about to visit a potentially harmful website.

Two things to keep in mind

- Don't _____ anything you wouldn't want broadcast to the entire world.

- The 'Golden Rule' of life is to treat others as you would like to be treated.

_____ information about one's identity should not be posted or shared on social media. Phone numbers, addresses, social security numbers, and family information are all included. This information can be used to recreate your _____ and should never be made public.

Make use of the _____ settings on the social media website. These can be used to control who can post information to your wall as well as who can see what is posted on it. Let's face it: there are some things you don't mind if your family and close friends know about, but you don't necessarily want your coworkers to find out about them through online posts.

Be positive.

Be cautious about what you post on any social media _____. Posting something _____ about someone hurts their character and opens the door for them, or someone else, to do the same to you. If you are not in a good mood or are upset, think twice. What you post could be _____ to you or someone else. Once you've made a post, it's always there. Even if you delete the post, this remains true!

If you are in a bad social media _____ and are being harassed or bullied, you can report it to the social media company. They all have _____ in place to deal with people who _____ their websites. Make a note of these _____ and report them to the company. You may also save the life of another person.

9th Grade Word of The Day

Use the dictionary to write the definition
and divide the words for each day
below into syllables.

○ MONDAY WORD: *UNICYCLE*

EXAMPLE:

A unicycle is a vehicle that touches the ground
with only one wheel.

u-ni-cy-cle

TUESDAY WORD: **laborious**

WEDNESDAY WORD: **robust**

THURSDAY WORD: **hygiene**

FRIDAY WORD: **potpourri**

SATURDAY / SUNDAY WORD: **pandemonium**

Write Words In ABC Order

For each word, find one synonym & one
antonym. (if none: write word + none)

A credit application is a lender's first step in acquiring consumer information. Informed decisions and information gathering are easier when they know more about you. A credit application is a request for credit from a lender.

9th Grade Life Skills   Credit Application

Name:	Date Birth:		SSN:

Current Address:			Phone:

City:	State:	ZIP:	

Own Rent (Please circle)	Monthly payment or rent:	How long?

Previous Address:

City:	State:	ZIP:	

Owned Rented (Please circle)	Monthly payment or rent:	How long?

Employment Information

Current Employer:	How long?

Employer Address:	Phone:

Position:	Hourly Salary (Please circle)	Annual Income:

Previous Employer:

Address:	How long?

Phone:	E-mail:	Fax:

Position:	Hourly Salary (Please circle)	Annual Income:

Name and relationship of a relative not living with you:

Address:

City:	State:	ZIP:	Phone:

Co-Applicant Information, if for a joint account

Name:	Date Birth:		SSN:

Current Address:			Phone:

City:	State:	ZIP:	

Own Rent (Please circle)	Monthly payment or rent:	How long?

Previous Address:

City:	State:	ZIP:	

Owned Rented (Please circle)	Monthly payment or rent:	How long?

Employment Information

Current Employer:	How long?

Employer Address:	Phone:

Position:	Hourly Salary (circle)	Annual Income:

Previous Employer:

Address:

Phone:	E-mail:	Fax:

Position:	Hourly Salary (circle)	Annual Income:

Name and relationship of a relative not living with you:

Address:

City:	State:	ZIP:	Phone:

Credit Cards

Name	Account No.	Current Balance	Monthly Payment

Mortgage Company

Account No.:	Address:

Auto Loans

Auto Loans	Account No.	Balance	Monthly Payment

Other Loans, Debts, or Obligations

Description	Account No.	Amount

Other Assets or Sources of Income

	Monthly Value: $
	Monthly Value: $

I/We authorize _____ to verify information provided on this form regarding credit and employment history.

Signature of Applicant	Date

Signature of Co-Applicant, if for joint account	Date

9th Grade Science: Different Blood Types

compatible	transfusion	recipient's	antibodies	survive
donate	bloodstream	eight	negative	antigens

What comes to mind when you think of blood? It may be the color red, a hospital, or even a horror film! Blood is

something that your body requires to _____, regardless of how you feel about it. Did you realize,

though, that not everyone has the same blood type? There are _____ different kinds in total! The letters A,

B, and O, as well as positive or _____ signs, distinguish these blood types. O+, O-, A+, A-, B+, B-,

AB+, and AB- are the eight blood types.

What Is the Importance of Blood Types?

Don't be concerned if your blood type differs from that of others! There is no such thing as a better or healthier

blood type. The sole reason to know your blood type is in case you need to _____ or give blood to

someone in an emergency. A blood _____ is a process of transferring blood from one

person to another.

Blood transfusions are only effective when the donor's blood is _____ with the

_____ blood. Some blood types don't mix well because the body produces antibodies to

fight off any unfamiliar _____ that enter the _____. Antibodies act as warriors

in your blood, guarding you against alien intruders. Assume you have Type A blood, which contains A antigens

solely, and someone with Type B blood wishes to donate blood to you. Your body does not recognize B antigens;

thus, _____ are produced to combat them! This has the potential to make you sick. As a result,

people with Type A blood should only receive blood from those with Type A blood or Type O blood, as O blood

lacks both A and B antigens.

9th Grade Math: Look It Up! Pop Quiz

Learn some basic vocabulary words that you will come across again and again in the course of your studies in algebra. By knowing the definitions of most algebra words, you will be able to construct and solve algebra problems much more easily.

Find the answer to the questions below by *looking up each word. (The wording can be tricky. Take your time.)*

1. improper fraction
   a. a fraction that represents both positive and negative numbers that has a value more than 1
   b. a fraction in which the numerator is greater than the denominator, is always 1 or greater
   c. a fraction that the denominator is equal to the numerator

2. equivalent fraction
   a. a fraction that has a DIFFERENT value as a given fraction
   b. a fraction that has the SAME value as a given fraction
   c. a fraction that has an EQUAL value as a given fraction

3. simplest form of fraction
   a. an equivalent fraction for which the only common factor of the numerator and denominator is 1
   b. an equivalent fraction for which the only least factor of the denominator is -1
   c. an equal value fraction for which the only common factor of the numerator and denominator is -1

4. mixed number
   a. the sum of a positive fraction and a reciprocal
   b. the sum of a whole number and a proper fraction
   c. the sum of a variable and a fraction

5. reciprocal
   a. a number that can be multiplied by another number to make 1
   b. a number that can be divided by another number to make 10
   c. a number that can be subtracted by another number to make -1

6. percent
   a. a ratio that compares a number to 100
   b. a percentage that compares a number to 0.1
   c. a 1/2 ratio that equals a number to 100

7. sequence

    a. a set of addition numbers that follow a operation

    b. a set of letters & numbers divided by 5 that makes a sequence

    c. a set of numbers that follow a pattern

8. arithmetic sequence

    a. a sequence where ONE term is found by dividing or subtracting the exact same number to the previous term

    b. a sequence where NO term is found by multiplying the exact same number to the previous term

    c. a sequence where EACH term is found by adding or subtracting the exact same number to the previous term

9. geometric sequence

    a. a sequence where each term is found by multiplying or dividing by the exact same number to the previous term

    b. a sequence where each term is divided or subtracted by the same fraction to the previous term

    c. a sequence where each term is solved by adding or dividing by a different number to the previous term

10. order of operations

    a. the procedure to follow when simplifying a numerical expression

    b. the procedure to follow when adding any fraction by 100

    c. the procedure to follow when simplifying an equation with the same answer

11. variable expression

    a. a mathematical phrase that contains numbers and operation symbols

    b. a mathematical phrase that contains variables, addition, and operation sequence

    c. a mathematical phrase that contains variables, numbers, and operation symbols

12. absolute value

    a. a whole number on the number line from one to zero

    b. the distance a number is from zero on the number line

    c. the range a number is from one on the number line

13. integers

    a. a set of numbers that equal to fractions line variables

    b. a set of numbers that includes equal numbers and their difference

    c. a set of numbers that includes whole numbers and their opposites

14. x-axis

    a. the horizontal number line that, together with the y-axis, establishes the coordinate plane

    b. the vertical number line that, together with the y-axis, establishes the coordinate plane

    c. both horizontal & vertical number line that, together with the y-axis, establishes the coordinate plane

15. y-axis

    a. the horizontal number line that, together with the x-axis, establishes the coordinate plane

    b. the vertical number line that, together with the x-axis, establishes the coordinate plane

    c. the vertical number line that, together with the x or y-axis, establishes the coordinate plane

16. coordinate plane

    a. plane formed by two number lines (the horizontal x-axis and the vertical y-axis) intersecting at their zero points

    b. plane formed by three number line (the vertical y-axis and the horizontal x-axis) intersecting at their two points

    c. plane formed by one number line (the horizontal y-axis and the vertical x-axis) intersecting at their -1 points

17. quadrant

    a. three sections on the axis plane formed by the intersection of the x-axis and the y-axis

    b. one of four sections on the coordinate plane formed by the intersection of the x-axis and the y-axis

    c. one of two sections on the four plane formed by the intersection of the x-axis

18. ordered pair

    a. a pair of integer number sets that gives the range of a point in the axis plane. Also known as the "x-axis" of a point.

    b. a pair of equal numbers that gives the range of a point in the axis plane. Also known as the "y-axis" of a point.

    c. a pair of numbers that gives the location of a point in the coordinate plane. Also known as the "coordinates" of a point.

19. x-coordinate

    a. the number that indicates the position of a point to the left or right of the y-axis

    b. the number that indicates the range of a point to the left ONLY of the y-axis

    c. the number that indicates the range of a point to both sides of the x-axis

20. y-coordinate

    a. the number that indicates the value of a point only above the x-axis

    b. the number that indicates the position of a point above or below the x-axis

    c. the number that indicates the value or range of a point only above the y-axis

21. inverse operations

    a. operations that divide evenly into each other

    b. operations that undo each other

    c. operations that equals to each other

22. inequality

    a. a math sentence that uses a symbol ($<$, $>$, $\leq$, $\geq$, $\neq$) to indicate that the left and right sides of the sentence hold values that are different

    b. a math sentence that uses a letter (x or y) to indicate that the left and right sides of the sentence hold values that are different

    c. a math sentence that uses both numbers and letters (1=x or 2=y) to indicate that the left and right sides of the sentence hold values that are different

23. perimeter

    a. the range around the outside or inside of a figure

    b. the distance around the outside of a figure

    c. the distance around the inside of a figure

24. circumference

    a. the distance around a circle

    b. the cube squared value around a circle

    c. the range around a square

25. area

    a. the number of circle units inside a 3-dimensional figure

    b. the number of triangle units inside a 2-dimensional figure

    c. the number of square units inside a 2-dimensional figure

26. volume

    a. the number of cubic squared units inside a 2-dimensional figure

    b. the number of cubic or circle units inside a 1-dimensional figure

    c. the number of cubic units inside a 3-dimensional figure

27. radius

    a. a line segment that runs from the center of the circle to somewhere on the circle

    b. a line segment that runs from the middle of the circle to end of the circle

    c. a line segment that runs from the middle of the square to start of the square

28. chord

    a. a circle distance that runs from somewhere on the far left to another place on the circle

    b. a line around a circle that runs from somewhere on the right to another place on the circle

    c. a line segment that runs from somewhere on the circle to another place on the circle

29. diameter

    a. a thin line that passes through the end of the circle

    b. a 1/2" line that passes through the top of the circle

    c. a chord that passes through the center of the circle

30. mean

    a. the sum of the data items added by the number of data items minus 2

    b. the sum of the data items divided by the number of data items

    c. the sum of the data items divdied by the number of even data items less than 1

31. median

    a. the middle data item found after sorting the data items in ascending order

    b. the first data item found after sorting the data items in descending order

    c. the middle & last data item found after sorting the data items in ascending order

32. mode

    a. the data item that occurs less than two times

    b. the data item that occurs when two or more numbers equal

    c. the data item that occurs most often

33. range

    a. the difference between the highest and the lowest data item

    b. the difference between the numbers less than 10 and the lowest number item 2

    c. the difference between the middle number and the lowest number item

34. outlier

    a. a data item that is much higher or much lower than all the other data items

    b. a data item that is much lower or less than all the other data items

    c. a data item that is always higher than 1 or less than all the other data items

35. ratio

    a. a comparison of two quantities by subtraction

    b. a comparison of two quantities by multiplication

    c. a comparison of two quantities by division

36. rate

    a. a ratio that has equal range and distance measured within the first unit set

    b. a ratio that has equal quantities measured in the same units

    c. a ratio that compares quantities measured in different units

37. proportion

    a. a statement (equation) showing two ratios to be equal

    b. a statement (property) showing the distance between two variables

    c. a statement (ratio) showing five or more ratios to be equal

38. outcomes

    a. possible answer when two numbers are the same

    b. possible results when the action is by division

    c. possible results of action

39. probability

    a. a ratio that explains the likelihood of two division problems with equal answers

    b. a ratio that explains the likelihood of an event

    c. a ratio that explains the likelihood of the distance and miles between to places

40. theoretical probability

    a. the probability of the highest favorable number of possible outcomes (based on what is not expected to occur).

    b. the ratio of the number of favorable outcomes to the number of possible outcomes (based on what is expected to occur).

    c. the probability of the lowest favorable number of possible outcomes (based on what is expected to occur when added by 5).

41. experimental probability

    a. the ratio of the number of times multiplied by the number of events that occur to the number of events times 5 (based on real experimental data).

    b. the ratio of the number of times by 2 when an event occurs to the number of times times 2 an experiment is done (based on real experimental data).

    c. the ratio of the number of times an event occurs to the number of times an experiment is done (based on real experimental data).

42. distributive property

    a. a way to simplify an expression that contains a single term being multiplied by a group of terms.

    b. a way to simplify an expression that contains a range of like terms being divided by a group of like terms.

    c. a way to simplify an expression that contains a equal like term being added by a group of terms.

43. term

    a. a number, a variable, or probability of an equal number and a variable(s)

    b. a number, a variable, or expression of a range of numbers and a variable(s)

    c. a number, a variable, or product of a number and a variable(s)

44. Constant

    a. a term with no variable + y part (i.e. 4+y)

    b. a term with no variable - x value (i.e. 8-x)

    c. a term with no variable part (i.e. a number)

45. Coefficient

    a. a number that multiplies a variable

    b. a number that divides a variable

    c. a number that subtracts a variable

46. Probability is the likelihood of something happening.

    a. True

    b. False

47. To calculate probability, you need to know how many possible options or _____ there are and how many right combinations you have.

    a. outcomes

    b. numbers

    c. fraction

48. _, _, and _ have two common factors: 2 and 4.

    a. 2, 6, and 9

    b. 12, 20, and 24

    c. 1,4, and 24

49. How do you write a polynomial expression?

    a. 3x2 -2x-10

    b. 32 -2x-+10y

    c. y+3x2 -2x-10

50. How can you simplify rational expression?

    a. eliminate all factors that are common of the numerator and the denominator

    b. eliminate only 1 factor that are common of the numerator and the denominator

    c. eliminate NO factors that are common of the numerator and the denominator

51. The slope intercept form is one of many forms that represents the linear relationship between two variables.

    a. True

    b. False

52. The slope intercept form equation is written as follows:

    a. $z = a x + b$

    b. $y = y x + m$

    c. $y = m x + b$

53. Simplifying radicals is that we do NOT remove the radicals from the denominator.

    a. True

    b. False

54. 2 1/3 is a mixed fraction.

    a. True

    b. False

55. The word _____ literally means 'per hundred.' We use this symbol - %.

    a. asterisk

    b. percent

    c. divide

56. less than or equal to symbol

    a. $\leq$

    b. $<$

    c. $\geq$

57. distance between points x and y

    a. $|x-y|$

    b. $|x+y|$

    c. $|x-y+x+y|$

58. greater than or equal to

    a. $<$

    b. $\leq$

    c. $\geq$

Order of Operations

The order of operations is a rule that specifies the correct sequence of steps to be taken when evaluating a mathematical expression. PEMDAS stands for Parentheses, Exponents, Multiplication and Division (from left to right), Addition and Subtraction (from left to right).

1) $(50 - 2) \div 3 - 7^2$

2) $3 \times (11 + 6) - 5^2$

3) $(28 - 2^2) \div (1 + 5)$

4) $(5 \times 4 - 7^2) + 3$

5) $(13 \times 6 + 7^2) + 4$

6) $(12 - 5)^2 + (20 \div 2)$

7) $(44 - 2^2) \div (4 + 4)$

8) $5 \times (9 + 2) - 5^2$

9) $(44 - 4) \div 8 + 5^2$

10) $(14 - 5)^2 + (8 \div 4)$

Quadrant Order

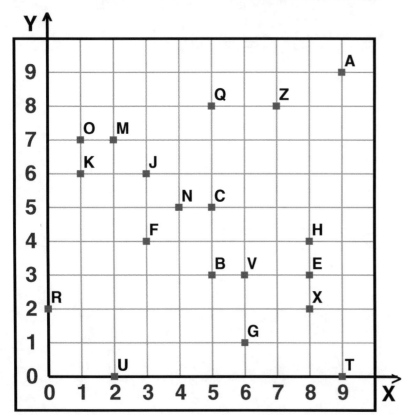

Tell what point is located at each ordered pair.

1) (8,3) _____   6) (1,6) _____

2) (9,9) _____   7) (4,5) _____

3) (8,2) _____   8) (0,2) _____

4) (6,3) _____   9) (9,0) _____

5) (6,1) _____   10) (5,8) _____

Write the ordered pair for each given point.

11) **B** _____   14) **Z** _____   17) **O** _____

12) **M** _____   15) **J** _____   18) **U** _____

13) **C** _____   16) **H** _____   19) **F** _____

Plot the following points on the coordinate grid.

20) **W** (7,6)   22) **L** (8,6)   24) **Y** (7,5)

21) **S** (7,1)   23) **D** (3,2)   25) **P** (4,8)

Score: _____

Date: _____

9th Grade Spelling Words
Unscramble

symphony	analysis	agriculture	twelfth	abundant	tendency
souvenir	technique	laborious	ambassador	sophomore	specific
symbol	specimen	aggressive	jealousy	absorption	journal
island	acceptable	syllable	absence	amateur	temperature

1. NECASEB   a _ _ _ _ _ e

2. PNSOABROTI   _ b _ _ _ t _ _ n

3. ABDNUTNA   _ _ _ _ d _ _ t

4. BLEATAPCEC   _ _ _ _ _ t a _ _ e

5. SLYBLELA   _ _ _ _ a _ _ e

6. BLOMYS   _ y _ _ _ l

7. OMHYPSYN   _ y _ _ _ _ n _

8. ENUTICQHE   t _ c _ _ _ _ _ _

9. EPTMERUATRE   _ e m _ _ _ _ _ _ _ e

10. EYNNDCET   _ _ n _ _ _ c _

11. GEEGSARVIS   _ g g _ _ s _ _ _ _

12. ARTEULICRUG   _ _ _ i c _ _ _ u _ _

13. UMTEAAR   a _ _ _ _ u _

14. AASBOARMSD   _ _ _ a _ _ a _ o _

15. LISASNAY   a _ _ _ y _ _ _

16. PMREHSOOO   _ _ p _ _ _ _ r _

17. VOESINUR   _ _ _ v _ n _ _

18. CSPFCIEI   _ _ _ c i _ _ _

19. SPCMENEI   _ p _ _ _ _ e _

20. DSLINA   i _ _ _ _ d

21. JSULYEOA   j e _ _ _ _ _ _

22. JRUOLNA   _ _ u _ _ a _

23. ASILOBURO   _ a b _ _ _ _ _ _

24. TELWTHF   _ _ e _ _ _ h

9th Grade Spelling Words Crossword

Across

1. We will meet at our summer ____ for the wedding
3. My father studied _____.
6. The _____ of the donors came as a surprise.
7. There was a growing ____ between the two sides.
8. The old home was in a _____ state.
9. The ____ between the villages was growing larger.

Down

2. The lamb ____ is nearly done cooking
4. The economic ____ appears to be working.
5. I've always wanted to play the _____.
10. The people were ____ of his motives.
11. Pass the ____ to me so that I can take my medicine.
12. The doctor told my grandma to take only one ____ a day.

VITAMIN   RESIDENCE
ANIMOSITY   WARY
XYLOPHONE   SHANK
CHASM   PODIATRY
SYRINGE   GENEROSITY
STIMULUS   RUINOUS

9th Grade Health: Check Your Symptoms

Healthy habits aid in the development of happy and healthy children as well as the prevention of future health issues such as diabetes, hypertension, high cholesterol, heart disease, and cancer.

Chronic diseases and long-term illnesses can be avoided by leading a healthy lifestyle. Self-esteem and self-image are aided by feeling good about yourself and taking care of your health.

Maintain a consistent exercise schedule.

No, you don't have to push yourself to go to the gym and do tough workouts, but you should be as active as possible. You can maintain moving by doing simple floor exercises, swimming, or walking. You can also remain moving by doing some domestic chores around the house.

What matters is that you continue to exercise. At least three to five times a week, devote at least twenty to thirty minutes to exercise. Establish a regimen and make sure you get adequate physical activity each day.

Be mindful of your eating habits.

You must continue to eat healthily in order to maintain a healthy lifestyle. Eat more fruits and vegetables and have fewer carbs, salt, and harmful fat in your diet. Don't eat junk food or sweets.

Avoid skipping meals since your body will crave more food once you resume eating. Keep in mind that you should burn more calories than you consume.

1. **I've got a pain in my head.**
   a. Stiff neck
   b. headache

2. **I was out in the sun too long.**
   a. Sunburn
   b. Fever

3. **I've got a small itchy lump or bump.**
   a. Rash
   b. Insect bite

4. **I might be having a heart attack.**
   a. Cramps
   b. Chest pain

5. **I've lost my voice.**
   a. Laryngitis
   b. Sore throat

6. **I need to blow my nose a lot.**
   a. Runny nose
   b. Blood Nose

7. **I have an allergy. I have a**
   a. Rash
   b. Insect bite

8. **My shoe rubbed my heel. I have a**
   a. Rash
   b. Blister

9. **The doctor gave me antibiotics. I have a/an**
   a. Infection
   b. Cold

10. **I think I want to vomit. I am**
    a. Nauseous
    b. Bloated

11. **My arm is not broken. It is**
    a. Scratched
    b. Sprained

12. **My arm touched the hot stove. It is**
    a. Burned
    b. Bleeding

13. **I have an upset stomach. I might**
    a. Cough
    b. Vomit

14. **The doctor put plaster on my arm. It is**
    a. Sprained
    b. Broken

15. **If you cut your finger it will**
    a. Burn
    b. Bleed

16. **I hit my hip on a desk. It will**
    a. Burn
    b. Bruise

17. **When you have hay-fever you will**
    a. Sneeze
    b. Wheeze

18. **A sharp knife will**
    a. Scratch
    b. Cut

9th Grade Grammar: some, any, a, an

A is used when the next word starts with a consonant sound.
AN is used when the next word starts with a vowel sound.
Some is generally used in positive sentences.
Any is generally used in negative sentences.

Rewrite the *scrambled words* so they form a complete *sentence*.

1. _____

   We · any · have · don't · apples.

2. _____

   make · some · lunch. · for · sandwiches · We · can

3. _____

   fridge. · in · There · the · isn't · any · milk

4. _____

   buy · I · to · tomatoes. · and · an · onion · need · some

5. _____

   carrots. · need · any · tomatoes · or · doesn't · She

6. _____

   have · any · we · potatoes? · Do

7. _____

   some · grapes. · We · have · don't · but · we · strawberries · any · have

8. _____

   There · any · isn't · sugar · in · bowl. · the

9. _____

   Can · a · I · banana, · have · please?

10. _____

on · there · the · any · apples · counter? · Are

11. _____

decision. · an · wasn't · easy · It

12. _____

a · She · forced · smile.

13. _____

an · I · appointment. · have

14. _____

horseman, · you · excellent · He · an · is · know.

15. _____

I · job, · an · easy · It's · expected. · like

16. _____

That · was · no-brainer. · a

17. _____

I · an · owe · me · think · you · explanation.

18. _____

at · the · tree. · foot · of · he · stopped · a · Suddenly

9th Grade Grammar: Is vs. Are

Use **is** if the noun is singular. If the noun is plural or there are multiple nouns, use **are**.

1. _____ Billy?
  1. Where are
  2. Where's

2. _____ in the bed.
  1. They're
  2. He's

3. _____ Mum and Dad?
  1. Where's
  2. Where are

4. _____ in the kitchen.
  1. She's
  2. They're

5. _____ Grandpa?
  1. Where are
  2. Where's

6. _____ in the garden.
  1. He's
  2. She's

7. _____ Lucy and Lilly?
  1. Where's
  2. Where are

8. _____ in the park.
  1. She's
  2. They're

9. _____ my sister?
  1. Where are
  2. Where's

10. _____ in her bedroom.
  1. He's
  2. She's

11. _____ pupils?
  1. Where are
  2. Where's

12. _____ at school.
  1. He's
  2. They're

9th Grade Math Vocabulary Quiz

1. algebraic equation

    a. an arrangement of items or events in which order does not matter

    b. a relation in which each member of the domain is paired with exactly one member of the range

    c. equality of two expressions formulated by applying to a set of variables the algebraic operations

2. direct evidence

    a. evidence that, if believed, directly proves a fact

    b. one or more sets of numbers on a number line or coordinate/grid paper

    c. cause and effect relationships that keep a system working within its limits

3. variable

    a. two mathematical expressions are equal

    b. a symbol (usually a letter) standing in for an unknown numerical value in an equation

    c. the job or action of individual parts working together to form a whole

4. scale factor

    a. a method of writing very large or very small numbers by using powers of 10

    b. a graph with points plotted to show a possible relationship between two sets of data

    c. the ratio of the lengths of two corresponding sides of two similar polygons or solids

5. computation

    a. an object, event, idea, feeling, time period

    b. Finding an answer by using mathematics or logic

    c. numerical value in an equation

6. equivalent

    a. two meanings, numbers, or quantities that are the same

    b. symbol which works as a placeholder for expression

    c. one on each side of an equals numbers

7. equation

    a. changeable a variable climate

    b. two math expressions are equal (indicated by the sign =)

    c. simply a statement in math in which two things equal

8. analyze

    a. a number tendency or inclination: prejudice

    b. to study or determine the nature and relationship of the parts of (something) by analysis

    c. a verbal subtraction argument; a regulated discussion of a problem between two opposing sides

9. **structure**
   a. the relation of a word to its base
   b. a noun in the form of the present participle of a verb
   c. the way that something is built, arranged, or organized

10. **summarize**
    a. the result so obtain a number
    b. 7 groups can be formed with 9 units
    c. Express the most important facts or ideas about something or someone in a short and clear form

11. **addends**
    a. the number resulting from the division
    b. answer after we divide one number by another
    c. A quantity to be added to another

12. **place value**
    a. divide one number by another
    b. multiplied by 100 between a test score and a standard value
    c. the basis of our entire number system

13. **difference**
    a. mathematical term that refers to the result of subtract
    b. The result of subtracting one number from another.
    c. quotient is the integer part of the result

14. **divisor**
    a. a number by which another number is to be divided.
    b. two variables, divided by a horizontal line

15. **numerator**
    a. expression that identifies factors to be multiplied
    b. number above the line of a fraction, showing the number of parts of the whole
    c. two or more numbers when multiplied together

16. **quotient**
    a. the result of an addition
    b. result of multiplying two or more values
    c. number obtained by dividing one number by another

Write sentences using words from above: Choose at least 5 different words.

1. _____

2. _____

3. _____

4. _____

5. _____

9th Grade Grammar: 8 Parts of Speech Matching

- **NOUN**. used to identify any of a class of people, places, or things
- **PRONOUN**. a word (such as I, he, she, you, it, we, or they) that is used instead of a noun or noun phrase
- **VERB**. a word used to describe an action, state, or occurrence
- **ADJECTIVE**. modify or describe a noun or a pronoun
- **ADVERB**. word that modifies (describes) a verb (she sings loudly), adverbs often end in -ly
- **PREPOSITION**. word or phrase that connects a noun or pronoun to a verb or adjective in a sentence
- **CONJUNCTION**. word used to join words, phrases, sentences, and clauses
- **INTERJECTION**. word or phrase that expresses something in a sudden or exclamatory way, especially an emotion

#		Question		Answer	
1	☐	Identify the noun.		verb	A
2	☐	Identify the verb.		mother, truck, banana	B
3	☐	What is an adjective?		Lion	C
4	☐	Three sets of nouns		conjunctions	D
5	☐	Three sets of adverbs		always, beautifully, often	E
6	☐	above, across, against		a word that describes nouns and pronouns	
7	☐	but, and, because, although		preposition	G
8	☐	Wow! Ouch! Hurrah!		preposition	H
9	☐	Mary and Joe **are** friends.		barked	
10	☐	Jane ran **around** the corner yesterday.		Interjection	J

Extra Credit: Write at least 3 examples of each: Interjection, Conjunction, Adverb & Preposition

_____

_____

_____

9th Grade Grammar:
Subjunctive Mood

Wishes, proposals, ideas, imagined circumstances, and assertions that are not true are all expressed in the subjunctive mood. The subjunctive is frequently used to indicate an action that a person hopes or wishes to be able to undertake now or in the future. In general, a verb in the subjunctive mood denotes a scenario or state that is a possibility, hope, or want. It expresses a conditional, speculative, or hypothetical sense of a verb.

When verbs of advice or suggestion are used, the subjunctive mood is utilized. After verbs of recommendation or advice, the subjunctive appears in a phrase beginning with the word -that.

Here are a few verbs that are commonly used in the subjunctive mood to recommend or advise.

- advise, ask, demand, prefer

1. Writers use the subjunctive mood to express _____ or _____conditions.

    a. imaginary or hoped-for

    b.

2. Which is NOT a common marker of the subjunctive mood?

    a.

    b. memories

3. Which is NOT an example of a hope-for verb?

    a. demand

    b. need

4. Subjunctive mood is used to show a situation is not _____.

    a. fictional or fabricated

    b. entirely factual or certain

5. Which of the below statements is written in the subjunctive mood?

    a. I wish I were a millionaire.

    b. What would you do with a million dollars?

6. The indicative mood is used to state facts and opinions, as in:

    a. My mom's fried chicken is my favorite food in the world.

    b. Smells, taste, chew

7. The imperative mood is used to give commands, orders, and instructions, as in:

    a. Eat your salad.

    b. I love salad!

8. The interrogative mood is used to ask a question, as in:

    a. Have you eaten all of your pizza yet?

    b. I ordered 2 slices of pizza.

9. The conditional mood uses the conjunction "if" or "when" to express a condition and its result, as in:

    a. Blue is my favorite color, so I paint with it often.

    b. If I eat too much lasagna, I'll have a stomach ache later.

10. The subjunctive mood is used to express wishes, proposals, suggestions, or imagined situations, as in:

    a. Yesterday was Monday, and I ate pizza.

    b. I prefer that my mom make pasta rather than tuna.

9th Grade Grammar: Linking Verbs

A linking verb links the topic of a phrase to a word that describes the subject, such as a condition or a relationship. They don't depict any action; instead, they serve to connect the subject to the rest of the phrase or sentence.

In a sentence, helping verbs always appear before the primary verb. They complete the structure of a phrase by adding information to the main verb. They can also help you understand how time is expressed in a sentence.

To connect nouns, pronouns, and adjectives, both the supporting and linking verb are utilized.

1. Which of the following examples best shows what a linking verb is?

    a. Shows action

    b. Connects a subject to the predicate

    c. Connects a noun and verb

2. How can you determine the difference between a helping verb and a linking verb?

    a. There is no difference between a helping verb and a linking verb.

    b. The helping verb is combined with an action verb.

    c. The helping verb or adverb shows action.

3. Which words belong to the category of state of being verbs?

    a. were, am, are, been

    b. flow, jump, bounce

    c. she, he, they, did

4. Which of the following examples does not connect subject and a predicate?

    a. Tiffany is an awesome student.

    b. She became the best mom ever!

    c. It danced quietly and smoothly.

5. What distinguishes a connecting verb from an action verb?

    a. It is an adjective.

    b. It shows no action.

    c. It shows action and no action.

6. The tomato smells rotten. Which is the linking verb in this sentence?

    a. rotten

    b. smells

    c. tomato

7. My brother is mad when he's hungry.

    a. is

    b. mad

    c. when

8. Identify the linking verb: The girl was frightened.

    a. girl

    b. was

    c. frightened

9. What is the linking verb in the sentence? Rob and Tony were class leaders.

    a. were

    b. class

    c. none

10. The Queen_____ busy laying eggs.

    a. is

    b. bee

    c. are

9th Grade Science: Kinetic Molecular Theory

The Kinetic Molecular Theory (KMT) is a model that explains the behavior of matter based on a set of postulates.

Pour yourself a drink of water. Using a dropper, add a few drops of red food coloring to the mixture. So, what happens next? The red food coloring drops should slowly work their way down the glass of water, spreading out to stain the entire glass crimson in color. What causes this to happen? It happens because both substances are made up of constantly moving molecules. One of the key concepts of the kinetic molecular theory is that these molecules have energy.

Liquids are fluid and can flow, which is one of their most noticeable characteristics. Liquids have a specific volume but no specific shape. Liquids are stated to have low compressibility, which means that packing liquid particles closer together is difficult.

Solids have well-defined shapes and volumes. Solid particles do travel, but just a short distance! Solid particles vibrate in situ because they have minimal kinetic energy. As a result, they are unable to flow like liquids.

Moving Matter

The ability to make changes in matter is defined as energy. When you lift your arm or take a step, for example, your body consumes chemical energy. Energy is utilized to move matter—you—in both circumstances. Any moving matter contains energy simply because it is moving. Kinetic energy is the energy of moving matter.

What are the 4 main points of kinetic molecular theory?

What are the 5 postulates of KMT?

What is the Kelvin scale and how does it relate to kinetic theory?

How does KMT explain Dalton's law?

Does pressure increase kinetic energy?

Extra Credit: Explain how kinetic energy is related to the mass and velocity of a particle.

9th Grade Science: Astronomy

Astronomy is an area of study that investigates celestial bodies such as stars, comets, planets, and galaxies in outer space. Astronomy is one of the oldest sciences, with evidence of individuals studying it dating back to Ancient Mesopotamia. Astronomy was also studied by later cultures such as the Greeks, Romans, and Mayans. However, all of these early scientists had to rely solely on their eyes to see space. They were only able to see so much. Scientists were able to see far further objects as well as have a clearer picture of closer objects like the moon and planets after the introduction of the telescope in the early 1600s.

Galileo Galilei improved the telescope significantly, enabling for near observations of the planets. He discovered several things, including Jupiter's four largest satellites (the Galilean moons) and sunspots.

Johannes Kepler was a well-known astronomer and mathematician who devised the planetary laws of motion, which explained how planets orbit the sun.

Using his principles of celestial motion and gravitation, **Isaac Newton** explained the physics of the solar system.

We are still producing big astronomical discoveries in the twenty-first century. Galaxies, black holes, neutron stars, quasars, and other objects have been discovered.

There are different fields in the science of astronomy. They include:

Observational Astronomy: What is the meaning of observational astronomy?

Theoretical Astronomy: What is the meaning of theoretical astronomy?

Solar Astronomy: What is the meaning of solar astronomy?

Planetary Astronomy: What is the meaning of planetary astronomy?

Stellar Astronomy: What is the meaning of stellar astronomy?

Extra Credit: What are 3 interesting facts about Isaac Newton?

9th Grade Science: Space

No one can hear you scream in space. This is due to the fact that space is devoid of air - it is a vacuum. In a vacuum, sound waves cannot travel. 'Outer space' begins roughly 100 kilometers above the Earth's surface, where the atmosphere that surrounds our planet dissipates. Space appears as a black blanket speckled with stars because there is no air to disperse sunlight and generate a blue sky.

Across

3. The 4 inner planets and 4 outer planets are separated by the _____ Belt.
4. The 4 inner planets are referred to as _____ planets because they are rocky and dense- Earth like
7. only about 1/2 the size of earth- tilted similar to earth- rusty surface- 2 moons
9. Revolves as rapidly as Jupiter- second largest planet- could float in water- Oh yeah...it has rings
10. Sideways rotation- retrograde rotation- has 11 very thin rings
13. _____ Solstice is when we have the longest amount of daylight for that year and the shortest night
16. The way we see the moon as it orbits around the sun and reflects the Sun's light
17. _____ Solstice is when we have the shortest amount of daylight for that year and the longest night

Down

1. The coming apart of an atom that gives off a lot of energy
2. The coming together of 2 atoms that releases a lot of energy - more than fission!
5. smallest planet- slowest rotation- magnetic
6. most like earth size wise- atmospheric pressure able to crush us- retrograde rotation
8. Fastest rotation (a little less than half an earth day)- largest planet- 29 years for 1 trip around the Sun- known also for Great Red Spot
11. Last planet in our solar system- Dark blue and windy-
12. Dwarf planet found just inside the Kuiper Belt- has a few moons- orbit actually crosses Neptune periodically
15. _____ Equinox is an occurrence in the fall where the daylight and nighttime are equivalent
17. the amount of moon that you can see is increasing
18. the amount of moon that you can see is decreasing
19. During a _____ Eclipse the shadow of the earth goes across the face of the moon

9th Grade Science: Organelles

Organelles are the inside elements of a cell that are responsible for all of the tasks that keep the cell healthy and alive. Each organelle has a distinct function. The word "organelle" means "small organ," and these tiny powerhouses are responsible for everything from defending the cell to repairing/healing, assisting in the development, removing waste products, and even reproduction. The function of each organelle is also influenced by the functions of other organelles. The cell will perish if any organelle fails to perform its function.

Many of the same types of organelles exist in both plant and animal cells, and they function in similar ways. Both plant and animal cells have a total of ten organelles.

Plant-like cells, on the other hand, are built solely for photosynthesis and utilize the rigid wall, as well as organelles that operate to generate energy from sunlight. Organelles in animal-like cells have a lot greater variety and capability.

Match each term with a definition.

#	Term		Definition	
1	nucleus		powerhouse of the cell	A
2	lysosomes		lipid synthesis	B
3	Golgi Apparatus		protein synthesis + modifications	C
4	Mitochondria		protein synthesis	D
5	SER		responsible for chromosome segregation	E
6	RER		where DNA is stored	F
7	Microtubules		modification of proteins; "post-office" of the cell	G
8	ribosomes		stores water in plant cells	H
9	peroxysomes		prevents excessive uptake of water, protects the cell (in plants)	I
10	cell wall		degradation of proteins and cellular waste	J
11	chloroplast		degradation of H2O2	K
12	central vacuole		site of photosynthesis	L

9th Grade Life Skills: A cash receipt is a printed confirmation of the amount of money received in a transaction involving the transfer of cash or cash equivalents.

Receipt No.   EXAMPLE

Write the date of the cash purchase

Date: _____

Write the cash amount received from the customer
Amount: _____

Write the item(s) purchase
Item: __Blue socks and purple shoes_____

Write who paid you
From: __Tommy Roberson_____

Write who the payment is for. Could be a company or individual name
To: __Kiddy Clothes Store_____

Write the name who received the payment

Write date you received the payment. In most cases, it can be the same day as the purchase date.

Received by: __Janet Miller_____   Date: _____

Pretend someone has just bought something from you, then fill out the receipt to reflect the transaction.

Receipt No.

Date: _____

Amount: _____

Item: _____

From: _____

To: _____

Received by: _____   Date: _____

Receipt No.

Date: _____

Amount: _____

Item: _____

From: _____

To: _____

Received by: _____   Date: _____

A job application's purposes is to gather information that will help shape the selection process, supply recruiters with the information they need to build interview questions, and ensure that you're qualified for the position and grasp the nature of the working relationship.

Application

Applicant

Name: Date:

Referral: Phone No.

Fax No.   Email:

Address:

Are You...

A U.S. Citizen?	☐ Yes	☐ No
Over 18 years old?	☐ Yes	☐ No
Licensed to drive?	☐ Yes	☐ No

Employment

Position: Department:

Type: ☐ Full-Time   ☐ Part-Time   ☐ Other (Seasonal/Temp):

Start Date: Starting Salary:

Current Employment: May we contact?   ☐ Yes   ☐ No

Education History

Education	School	Location	Years	Graduated?	Degree(s)
High School					
College					
Graduate					
Other Training/Classes:					
Workshops/Certifications:					

Employment History

Employer	Address	Position	Dates	Reason for Leaving

References

Reference	Relationship	Phone	Email	Address

Applicant Signature   Date

Shakespeare: Romeo and Juliet

Across

1. an enemy or opponent
2. something surrendered or subject to surrender as punishment for a crime, an offense, an error, or a breach of contract
3. loathsome; disgusting
7. to expel or banish a person from his or her country
8. to feel sorry for; regret
12. a small container, as of glass, for holding liquids
15. long and tiresome

Down

3. boldly courageous; brave; stout-hearted
5. to express disapproval of; scold; reproach
6. a musician, singer, or poet
9. an expression of grief or sorrow
10. to flood or to overwhelm
11. a malicious, false, or defamatory statement or report
13. infliction of injury, harm, humiliation, or the like, on a person by another who has been harmed by that person; violent revenge
14. to read through with thoroughness or care

VALIANT   LAMENT   SLANDER
MINSTREL   PERUSE
TEDIOUS   CHIDE   EXILE
VILE   FORFEIT   INUNDATE
REPENT   ADVERSARY   VIAL
VENGEANCE

AREA 51 WORDSEARCH

15 words in Wordsearch: 5 vertical, 5 horizontal, 5 diagonal. (10 reversed.)

Area 51, a classified United States Air Force military installation near Groom Lake in southern Nevada. Edwards Air Force Base in southern California is in charge of it. The facility has been the subject of numerous conspiracies involving **extraterrestrial life**, despite the fact that its only confirmed use is as a flight testing facility.

B	Q	V	X	N	Y	X	W	M	L	P	R	G	L	Y	O	E	P	I	N
U	Y	J	D	M	Y	C	G	K	Q	D	I	P	I	M	M	N	T	R	I
J	R	E	K	E	P	K	R	S	O	Z	D	H	I	J	N	N	G	E	L
X	J	E	T	Z	N	A	D	D	L	U	S	Q	S	A	H	O	H	T	B
V	G	O	T	W	M	N	E	J	U	K	H	X	B	E	U	X	M	S	O
N	Y	Q	K	E	M	I	I	F	D	S	H	S	Z	Y	C	H	T	N	G
K	K	Q	I	J	F	I	J	K	I	K	R	G	K	U	H	A	B	O	E
U	N	P	H	N	G	B	L	N	S	X	D	P	U	A	U	G	P	M	L
T	Q	H	R	D	M	U	E	G	S	Y	S	L	F	U	M	J	A	S	L
J	T	S	P	A	D	E	S	H	A	P	E	D	H	E	A	D	Y	D	I
W	J	O	L	T	R	N	E	M	N	E	E	R	G	D	N	G	I	O	V
S	D	P	I	G	A	O	Z	X	B	Y	M	S	G	R	O	M	Y	O	S
S	D	V	M	Z	V	I	D	X	L	T	R	S	E	L	I	F	X	W	N
P	S	H	W	A	G	T	J	W	E	A	H	U	X	N	D	Z	J	T	I
X	J	R	U	O	L	C	C	S	E	Y	E	E	U	L	B	T	O	A	K
H	F	B	O	W	D	U	R	O	Q	E	Z	T	W	J	J	J	C	L	P
X	K	V	V	X	F	D	N	Q	Q	E	I	J	M	U	S	F	C	F	O
V	O	P	O	J	L	B	Q	O	B	V	C	M	L	F	K	U	E	S	H
B	Z	Q	X	X	F	A	J	D	E	E	H	K	C	O	L	I	J	W	K
N	J	T	P	P	S	F	G	W	Q	W	K	Y	C	S	A	U	D	K	B

Humanoid
Xfiles
Spaceship

Spade Shaped Head
Ufos
Diminutive

Flatwoods Monster
Greenish
Abduction

No Ears
Hopkinsville Goblin
Blue Eyes

Grey Skinned
Green Men
Lockheed

9th Grade Music: Orchestra Vocabulary Words

Score: _____

Date: _____

Unscramble the names of the instruments found in the orchestra.

saxaphone	woodwind	xylophone	cello	drums	clarinet
violin	oboe	flute	cymbals	bassoon	percussion
double bass	trumpet	piano	brass	strings	trombone
timpani	harp	french horn	conductor		

1. ltuef   _ _ _ t _

2. oilinv   _ _ o _ i _

3. eoob   _ _ o _

4. rehncf rohn   _ _ _ _ _ h   _ _ _ n

5. sboosan   _ _ s _ o _ _

6. ecrantli   _ l _ _ _ n _ _

7. udsmr   _ _ u _ _

8. natimpi   _ i _ p _ _ _

9. grstisn   _ _ r _ _ g _

10. oodwdnwi   _ o _ _ _ i _ _

11. arssb   _ _ _ _ s

12. picuoersns   p e _ _ _ _ s _ _ _

13. olecl   _ _ l _ _

14. arph   _ _ _ p

15. oedlbu sbsa   _ o _ _ l _   _ _ _ _

16. rettupm   t _ _ _ _ e _

17. tnboeorm   t _ o _ _ _ _ _

18. xphynleoo   _ _ _ _ _ h _ n _

19. lmysabc   _ _ m _ a _ _

20. rtcudoocn   _ _ _ _ _ _ _ o r

21. oainp   _ _ a _ _

22. poeahaxsn   s _ _ a _ _ _ _ _

There are many forms of energy. Research each source and in 1 or 2 sentences, explain the advantages and or disadvantages for each.

ENERGY

ELECTRICAL
ENERGY

ENERGY
CROP

NON-RENEWABLE
ENERGY

ENERGY
CONSUMPTION

ENERGY
CONSERVATION

ENERGY
DEVELOPMENT

SUSTAINABLE
LIFE

NATURAL
GATEWAY

TIDAL
ENERGY

WAVE
ENERGY

BATTERY
ENERGY

ENERGY
PYRAMID

ENERGY
SAVING

WIND
ENERGY

SOLAR
ENERGY

GEOTHERMAL
ENERGY

HYDROELECTRIC
ENERGY

RENEWABLE
ENERGY

BIOMASS
ENERGY

ECO
ENERGY

NATURAL
GAS

ENERGY
SUPPLY

CLEAN
ENERGY

BIO
DIESEL

FOSSIL
FUEL

ENERGY
RESOURCE

ENERGY
RECYCLING

GREENHOUSE

POPULATION
GROWTH

GLOBAL
WARMING

SOLAR POWER
SYSTEM

SOLAR
CELL

ENERGY
EFFICIENCY HOUSE

HYDRO
POWER

BIOGAS

NUCLEAR
POWER

Energy Sources

Match Elements of the Periodic Table

The periodic table is the most important source of chemistry information. It arranges all of the known elements in a useful array. Elements are arranged in increasing atomic number order from left to right and top to bottom. The periodic table lists all known elements, grouping those with similar properties together.

A substance that cannot be broken down into another substance is referred to as an element. There are approximately 100 elements, each with its own atom type. Atoms of at least one or more elements can be found in everything in the universe. The periodic table lists all known elements, grouping those with similar properties together.

Match the chemical element in the first column with the correct abbreviation from the second column. Write the corresponding letter for each element in the box.

1	☐	Dubnium	Rg	A
2	☐	Seaborgium	Cn	B
3	☐	Bohrium	Ts	C
4	☐	Hassium	Mc	D
5	☐	Meitnerium	Db	E
6	☐	Darmstadtium	Bh	F
7	☐	Roentgenium	Hs	G
8	☐	Copernicium	Sg	H
9	☐	Nihonium	Fl	I
10	☐	Flerovium	Ds	J
11	☐	Moscovium	Nh	K
12	☐	Livermorium	Og	L
13	☐	Tennessine	Lv	M
14	☐	Oganesson	Mt	N

9th Grade HEALTH: Foods and Nutrition

SCORE:_____

DATE: _____

Nutrition aids in the maintenance of a healthy immune system. Because our immune system is our first line of defense against diseases, poor nutrition can make us more susceptible to them.

Across

1. blood disorder caused by lack of iron
3. fat-like substance in cells needed for many body processes
6. a condition in which the body has too little water
9. a protein that transports oxygen in the blood
12. a set of directions for making a food or beverage
13. the amount of space an ingredient takes up
14. the amount or number of servings a recipe makes

Down

2. essential nutrient that is the body's main source of energy
4. in baking, blending fat and sugar thoroughly together before adding other ingredients
6. too little of an essential nutrient
7. the parts of fruits, vegetables, grains and legumes that cannot be digested
8. blood sugar, the body's basic fuel
10. poor nourishment resulting from a lack of nutrients
11. the rate at which the body uses nutrients to provide energy

VOLUME   CHOLESTEROL
ANEMIA   RECIPE
DEHYDRATION
DEFICIENCY   GLUCOSE
CREAMING   YIELD
METABOLISM
HEMOGLOBIN
MALNUTRITION   FIBER
CARBOHYDRATE

white	defends	cell-mediated	cells	Immune
external	Macrophages	signals	foreign	invading

Your immune system _____ you against harmful intruders. _____ responses occur when your body's immune system detects threats.

Your immune system, which detects and eliminates _____ invaders, provides this tremendous service. An immunological reaction occurs when your body's immune system detects _____ intruders. Your immune system is a great asset that selflessly protects you from antigens, or foreign intruders.

Immunity by Cells

Antibody-mediated immunity is one of your immune system's two arms. The other arm is _____ immunity, which helps the body get rid of undesired cells like infected, cancerous, or transplanted cells. _____ consume antigens in this sort of immunity. If you split down macrophages, you can remember it easily. Big indicates macro- and phages means 'eaters.' So macrophages are voracious consumers of antigens. The macrophage then chews up the antigen and displays the fragments on its surface.

When helper T cells encounter macrophages, they give out _____ that activate other _____ blood _____, such as cytotoxic or killer T cells. These killer T cells multiply fast, forming an army ready to battle and eliminate the _____ cell that prompted the immune response.

9th Grade Grammar:
Contractions Multiple Choice

Simply put, you replace the letter(s) that were removed from the original words with an apostrophe when you make the contraction.

1. Here is
   a. Here's
   b. Heres'

2. One is
   a. Ones'
   b. One's

3. I will
   a. Il'l
   b. I'll

4. You will
   a. You'll
   b. Yo'ill

5. She will
   a. She'll
   b. She'ill

6. He will
   a. He'ill
   b. He'll

7. It will
   a. It'ill
   b. It'll

8. We will
   a. We'll
   b. We'ill

9. They will
   a. They'ill
   b. They'll

10. That will
    a. That'l
    b. That'll

11. There will
    a. There'ill
    b. There'll

12. This will
    a. This'll
    b. This'ill

13. What will
    a. What'ill
    b. What'll

14. Who will
    a. Who'll
    b. Whol'l

9th Grade History: Henry VIII

Read about Henry VIII and answer whatever questions you can.

Read here: https://www.britannica.com/biography/Henry-VIII-king-of-England (or Google "**Britannica.com Henry VIII**")

1. **Henry only became king because his elder brother died young.**
   a. True
   b. False

2. **The Tudors were an English royal dynasty in the 15th century.**
   a. True
   b. False

3. **The young Henry 8th was a weak and sickly young man.**
   a. True
   b. False

4. **His father, Henry 7th, was an unpopular king.**
   a. True
   b. False

5. **Henry tried to emulate his father's way of ruling.**
   a. True
   b. False

6. **Henry married Catherine of Aragon, his brother's wife.**
   a. True
   b. False

7. **Henry had a good relationship with his father-in-law, Ferdinand 2**
   a. True
   b. False

8. **Europe's unity at the time depended on a balance of power between Spain and France.**
   a. True
   b. False

9. **Cardinal Wolsey was a trusted advisor and friend of Henry 8.**
   a. True
   b. False

10. **Many thought that it was actually Wolsey who ruled England.**
    a. True
    b. False

11. **Henry disapproved of Wolsey's ambition of becoming the pope.**
    a. True
    b. False

12. **When Charles 5 came to power, Henry lost influence in Europe.**
    a. True
    b. False

13. **Wolsey lost power when his plans damaged English trade with the Netherlands**
    a. True
    b. False

14. **Ferdinand 2 of Aragon was Queen Catherine's grandfather.**
    a. True
    b. False

15. **By 1523 the English were becoming increasingly dissatisfied with the king.**

    a. True

    b. False

16. **By 1527 Wolsey's policies had brought England to the point of bankruptcy.**

    a. True

    b. False

17. **"The King's Matter" was a plan to break away from the Catholic Church.**

    a. True

    b. False

18. **Henry was a strong believer in the Catholic Church.**

    a. True

    b. False

19. **Both the pope and Henry believed he had been wrong to marry Catherine of Aragon.**

    a. True

    b. False

20. **The pope refused to annul Henry's marriage because a previous pope had allowed it.**

    a. True

    b. False

21. **Henry got rid of Wolsey because he couldn't find a solution to his marital problem.**

    a. True

    b. False

22. **Thomas More promised to help the king divorce.**

    a. True

    b. False

23. **Henry, with Thomas More, tried to preserve Catholicism in England.**

    a. True

    b. False

24. **Thomas More organized the break from Rome in 1532.**

    a. True

    b. False

25. **The split from Rome made the king the leader of the new church.**

    a. True

    b. False

26. **The king converted to protestantism because he no longer believed in the Catholic Church.**

    a. True

    b. False

27. **Henry created a completely new church based on his own religious beliefs.**

    a. True

    b. False

28. **Henry was a great admirer of Luther and used him for inspiration.**

    a. True

    b. False

29. **Henry was excommunicated by the pope.**

    a. True

    b. False

30. **Henry raised money by selling the Catholic Church's lands in England.**

    a. True

    b. False

Languages & Nationalities

Learn how to *look up* words in a *Spanish-English dictionary or online. Carefully* choose the correct Spanish spelling for each listed below.

1. Albanian
    a. albanés
    b. noruego

2. Arabian
    a. árabe
    b. rumano

3. Bosnian
    a. bosnio
    b. árabe

4. Bulgarian
    a. portugués
    b. búlgaro

5. Czech
    a. portugués
    b. checo

6. Danish
    a. noruego
    b. danés

7. Dutch
    a. holandés
    b. ucraniano

8. Hebrew
    a. hebreo
    b. húngaro

9. Hungarian
    a. húngaro
    b. irlandés

10. Irish
    a. árabe
    b. irlandés

11. Norwegian
    a. noruego
    b. esloveno

12. Polish
    a. sueco
    b. polaco

13. Portuguese
    a. danés
    b. portugués

14. Romanian
    a. rumano
    b. checo

15. Slovenian
    a. esloveno
    b. bosnio

16. Swedish
    a. albanés
    b. sueco

17. Turkish
    a. turco
    b. albanés

18. Ukrainian
    a. rumano
    b. ucraniano

Score: _____

9th Grade Geography: Landform

Date: _____

A landform is a natural or man-made feature of the Earth's or another planet's solid surface. A given terrain is made up of landforms, and their arrangement in the landscape is known as topography.

1. Lakes are an inland body of water, usually fresh
   a. True
   b. False

2. A sea is the direction from which a river flows
   a. True
   b. False

3. A delta is the land deposited at the mouth of a river
   a. True
   b. False

4. What landform is surrounded by water on three sides?
   a. An island
   b. A peninsula

5. A river is a narrow man-made channel of water that joins other bodies of water
   a. True
   b. False

6. The mouth is where a river flows into a larger body of water.
   a. True
   b. False

7. Which of the following is NOT a landform?
   a. An island
   b. A river

8. Downstream is the direction toward which a river flows.
   a. True
   b. False

9. A sea is a large area of salt water smaller than an ocean.
   a. True
   b. False

10. A bay is land deposited at the mouth of a river.
    a. True
    b. False

11. How are a valley and a canyon alike?
    a. They are both tall landforms.
    b. They are both low landforms.

12. A canal is a man-made channel of water that joins other bodies of water.
    a. True
    b. False

13. A lake is a place where a river begins.
    a. True
    b. False

14. Which types of landforms are always flat?
    a. Plateaus and plains
    b. Hills and peninsulas

9th Grade Geography: Know Your World

Test your knowledge of global, national, and local geography, as well as the environment.

1. Spain can be found in which continent
    a. Europe
    b. New Zealand
    c. Bogota

2. Uganda can be found in which continent
    a. Canberra
    b. Africa
    c. Lake Taupo

3. Uruguay can be found in which continent
    a. South America
    b. Atlantic Ocean
    c. Bogota

4. Beijing is the capital city of
    a. China
    b. Samoa
    c. New York

5. Honshu is an island of what country
    a. Japan
    b. Suva
    c. New York

6. Apia is the capital city of
    a. Bogota
    b. Samoa
    c. Brasilia

7. The Amazon River can be found in which continent
    a. Suva
    b. Buenos Aires
    c. South America

8. The Southern Alps can be found in which country
    a. Portugal
    b. New Zealand
    c. Brasilia

9. The Andes Mountains can be found in which continent
    a. Brasilia
    b. South America
    c. Berlin

10. Lines of longitude run
    a. Vertical - North to South
    b. Wellington
    c. Samoa

11. Lines of latitude run
    a. Horizontal - East to West
    b. Suva
    c. Italy

12. The ocean between the Americas and Europe and Africa is the
    a. Africa
    b. Italy
    c. Atlantic Ocean

13. The capital city of France is
    a. Bogota
    b. Paris
    c. Buenos Aires

14. The capital city of Germany is
    a. Berlin
    b. New Zealand
    c. Moscow

15. The capital city of Russia is
    a. Moscow
    b. Buenos Aires
    c. Paris

16. The capital city of the United States is
    a. Brasilia
    b. Washington D.C
    c. China

17. The capital city of Fiji is
    a. Suva
    b. Portugal
    c. Buenos Aires

18. Mt Everest can be found in what continent
    a. Asia
    b. Japan
    c. Wellington

19. Switzerland is a country in
    a. Europe
    b. Wellington
    c. Portugal

20. The capital city of Brazil is
    a. Japan
    b. China
    c. Brasilia

21. The capital city of Colombia is
    a. Spain
    b. Bogota
    c. Japan

22. The capital city of Argentina is
    a. Buenos Aires
    b. Portugal
    c. Bogota

23. Vietnam can be found in what continent
    a. Asia
    b. Berlin
    c. Vertical - North to South

24. Libya can be found in what continent
    a. Africa
    b. Bogota
    c. New York

25. Rome is the capital city of which European country
    a. Buenos Aires
    b. Italy
    c. Paris

26. Madrid is the capital city of which European country
    a. Brasilia
    b. Europe
    c. Spain

27. Lisbon is the capital city of which European country
    a. Samoa
    b. Portugal
    c. Buenos Aires

28. The Statue of Liberty can be found in what US city
    a. Italy
    b. New York
    c. Paris

29. The capital city of New Zealand is
    a. Canberra
    b. Wellington
    c. Washington D.C

30. The capital city of Australia is
    a. China
    b. Moscow
    c. Canberra

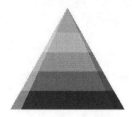

9th Grade Art: Roman Portrait Sculptures

Alexander	aristocrats	ancestral	shrine	rewarded
sculpture	pattern	mosaics	marble	artistic

Portrait _____ has been practiced since the beginning of Roman history. It was most likely

influenced by the Roman practice of creating _____ images. When a Roman man died, his family

made a wax sculpture of his face and kept it in a special _____ at home. Because these sculptures were

more like records of a person's life than works of art, the emphasis was on realistic detail rather than

_____ beauty.

As Rome became more prosperous and gained access to Greek sculptors, Roman _____

known as patricians began creating these portraits from stone rather than wax.

Roman sculpture was about more than just honoring the dead; it was also about honoring the living. Important

Romans were _____ for their valor or greatness by having statues of themselves erected and

displayed in public. This is one of the earliest of these types of statues that we've discovered, and the

_____ continued all the way until the Republic's demise.

The mosaic is the only form of Roman art that has yet to be discussed. The Romans adored mosaics and created

them with exquisite skill. The Romans created _____ of unprecedented quality and detail using cubes

of naturally colored _____. The floor mosaic depicting _____ the Great at the Battle of

Issus is probably the most famous Roman mosaic.

9th Grade Art: Pop Art

In 1957, Richard Hamilton described the style, writing: "Pop art is: **popular, transient, expendable, low-cost, mass-produced, young, witty, sexy, gimmicky, glamorous and big business**."

humor	events	spread	founded	activists
Gallery	artists	pioneer	vibrant	celebrity

Pop art was _____ in the mid-1950s in Britain by the Independent Group, a group of painters, sculptors, writers, and critics. It quickly spread to the United States. Much of the movement's origins can be traced back to a cultural revolution led by _____, thinkers, and _____ who sought to restructure a conformist social order. Many believe that U.K. Pop _____ Richard Hamilton's 1956 collage is responsible for the movement's rapid _____. Just what is it that makes today's homes so different, so appealing? Its appearance in London's Whitechapel _____ marked the official start of the cultural phenomenon.

Images and icons from popular media and products were used in pop art. This included commercial items such as soup cans, road signs, _____ photos, newspapers, and other items common in the commercial world. Brand names and logos were also used.

Pop art is distinguished by its use of _____, bright colors. The primary colors red, yellow, and blue were prominent pigments in many well-known works, particularly in Roy Lichtenstein's body of work.

One of the most important aspects of Pop art was _____. Artists use the subject matter to make a point about current _____, mock fads, and question the status quo.

9th Grade History Reading Comprehension: George Washington

You've probably seen him on a one-dollar bill. The capital of the United States is named after him.

George Washington was born on February 22, 1732, and died on December 14, 1799. As the son of wealthy plantation owners, he grew up in Colonial Virginia. A plantation is a large farm that is tended by a large number of people. George's father died when he was 11 years old, so he was raised primarily by his older brother, who ensured he received a basic education and learned how to be a gentleman. George's teeth had deteriorated over time, necessitating the use of dentures (fake teeth). They eventually turned a dingy brown color, and many people assumed they were made of wood, but they weren't. Imagine attempting to eat corn on the cob with wooden teeth.

George married the widow Martha Custis, who had two children from her previous marriage when he was an adult. A widow is someone whose husband has died, which is why she was able to marry George later in life. George became a plantation owner while also serving in the Virginia legislature, which meant he helped write and pass laws in Virginia. He was a very busy man!

The United States had not yet been formed at this point, and the British still ruled and owned the colonies. George and his fellow plantation owners became enraged because they felt they were being treated unfairly by their British rulers. A group of people from each town or colony met and decided that the colonies would fight the British together.

George Washington was elected as the first President of the United States of America in 1789. He had the option of becoming king, but he believed that no one should be in power for too long. A president in the United States is elected or chosen by popular vote, and George Washington decided not to run for reelection after his second term. Almost all American presidents followed in his footsteps, but the two-term (or eight-year) limit was not established until the 1950s.

George Washington served as president during peaceful times, and he was instrumental in establishing the new government and leadership of the United States. He was also a member of the leadership that aided in the adoption of the Constitution. The United States Constitution is the law of the land, and it guarantees the people of our country basic freedoms. However, freedom does not imply the ability to do whatever you want. Even free countries have laws and rules that must be followed.

Washington caught a cold just a few years after leaving the presidency. He became ill quickly with a cold and died on December 14, 1799.

Fun Facts

He was the only president who was elected unanimously.

He never served as president in the capital named after him, Washington, D.C. The capital was in New York City during his first year, then moved to Philadelphia, Pennsylvania.

He stood six feet tall, which was unusual for the 1700s.

George Washington did not have wooden teeth, but he did wear ivory dentures.

In his will, Washington freed his slaves.

1. George Washington was born on _____.
   a. 02-22-1732
   b. February 24, 1732

2. The United States Constitution is the law of the _____.
   a. land
   b. world

3. George's _____ had deteriorated.
   a. teeth
   b. feet

4. George Washington can be seen on a _____.
   a. one-dollar bill
   b. five-dollar bill

5. George's father died when he was 20 years old.
   a. True
   b. False

6. George was a plantation owner.
   a. True
   b. False

7. George married the widow _____.
   a. Martha Custis
   b. Mary Curtis

8. In his will, Washington freed his _____.
   a. children
   b. slaves

9. George served in the _____ legislature.
   a. Virginia
   b. Maryland

10. George Washington was elected as the _____ President of the USA.
    a. forth
    b. first

11. A widow is someone whose husband has died.
    a. True
    b. False

12. George died on December 14, 1699.
    a. True
    b. False

13. George grew up in _____.
    a. Washington DC
    b. Colonial Virginia

14. The capital of the United States is named after George.
    a. True
    b. False

15. A plantation is a town that is tended by a large number of officials.
    a. True
    b. False

16. Washington caught a _____ just a few years after leaving the presidency.
    a. cold
    b. flight

9th Grade History Reading Comprehension: John Hanson

Many people do not realize that when we refer to the President of the United States, we are actually referring to presidents elected under the United States Constitution. Everyone knows that George Washington was the first president in that sense. However, the predecessor to the Constitution, the Articles of Confederation, also called for a president, albeit one with greatly limited powers. Under the Articles of Confederation, eight men were appointed to one-year terms as president. Under the Articles of Confederation, John Hanson became the first President of the United States in Congress Assembled in November 1781.

Many argue that John Hanson, rather than George Washington, was the first President of the United States, but this is not entirely correct. The United States had no executive branch under the Articles of Confederation. Within the Confederation Congress, the President of Congress was a ceremonial position. Although the job required Hanson to deal with correspondence and sign official documents, it was not the type of work that any President of the United States would have done under the Constitution.

Hanson disliked his job as well, finding it tedious and wishing to resign. Unfortunately, the Articles of Confederation did not account for succession, so his departure would have left Congress without a President. So he stayed in office because he loved his country and felt obligated to do so.

During his tenure, which lasted from November 5, 1781 to November 3, 1782, he was able to remove all foreign troops and flags from American soil. He also established the Treasury Department, as well as the first Secretary of War and Foreign Affairs Department. He led the flight to ensure the statehood of the Western Territories beyond the Appalachian Mountains, which had previously been controlled by some of the original thirteen colonies.

What's most intriguing is that Hanson is also credited with establishing Thanksgiving Day as the fourth Thursday of November.

Being the first person in this position as President of Congress was not an easy task. So it's amazing that Hanson was able to accomplish so much. Furthermore, instead of the current four-year term, Presidents under the Articles of Confederation served only one year. So, accomplishing anything in such a short period of time was a great accomplishment.

Hanson played an important role in the development of United States Constitutional History, which is often overlooked but is undeniably true. Hanson is frequently referred to as the "forgotten first President." According to Seymour Weyss Smith's biography of him, John Hanson, Our First President, the American Revolution had two primary leaders: George Washington in the military sphere and John Hanson in the political sphere. Despite the fact that one position was purely ceremonial and the other was more official, statues of both men can be found in the United States Capitol in Washington, D.C.

Hanson died at the age of 62 on November 15, 1783.

1. Hanson served from November 5, 1781 until December 3, 1782
   a. True
   b. False

2. Hanson really LOVED his job.
   a. True
   b. False

3. Under the Articles of Confederation, the United States had no _____.
   a. executive branch
   b. congress office

4. The President of Congress was a _____ position within the Confederation Congress.
   a. senate
   b. ceremonial

5. In November 1781, Hanson became the first President of the United States in Congress Assembled, under the _____.
   a. Articles of Congress
   b. Articles of Confederation

6. ____ men were appointed to serve one year terms as president under the Articles of Confederation.
   a. Eight
   b. Two

7. Hanson was able to remove all _____ troops from American lands.
   a. foreign
   b. USA

8. Hanson is also responsible for establishing _____ as the fourth Thursday in November.
   a. Christmas Day
   b. Thanksgiving Day

9. Instead of the four year term that current Presidents serve, Presidents under the Articles of Confederation served only ___ year.
   a. one
   b. three

10. Hanson died on November 15, 1783 at the age of ____.
    a. 64
    b. sixty-two

11. Both George Washington and Hanson are commemorated with ____ in the United States Capitol in Washington, D.C.
    a. houses
    b. statues

12. George Washington in the military sphere and John Hanson in the ____ sphere.
    a. presidential
    b. political

Cursive Writing Practice

I Love School

Life is good

I am powerful.

I am enough.

I've got this.

I am smart.

I am capable.

Cursive Writing Practice

Science Vocabulary Builder

If you need to, use a separate piece of paper for writing.

HEREDITY AND GENETICS

What exactly is genetics?
The study of genes and heredity is known as genetics. It investigates how living organisms, including humans, inherit characteristics from their parents.

Geneticists are scientists who study genetics.

What exactly are genes?
Genes are the fundamental units of heredity. They are made of DNA and are part of a larger structure known as a chromosome. Genes contain information that determines which characteristics an organism inherits from its parents. They determine things like the color of your hair, your height, and the color of your eyes.

What exactly are chromosomes?
Chromosomes are DNA and protein-based structures found inside cells. The information contained within chromosomes functions as a recipe, instructing cells on how to function. Humans have 23 pairs of chromosomes in each cell, for a total of 46 chromosomes. The number of chromosomes in other plants and animals varies. A garden pea, for example, has 14 chromosomes, whereas an elephant has 56.

What exactly is DNA?
The actual instructions contained within the chromosome are stored in a long molecule known as DNA. DNA is an abbreviation for deoxyribonucleic acid.

True or False: Diseases cannot be inherited through genes. Explain why or why not.

Write the definition of each word below.

Heredity:

Trait:

Recessive Trait:

Dominant Trait:

Allele:

Genotype:

Phenotype:

Homozygous:

Heterozygous:

Purebred:

Mutation:

EXTRA CREDIT BOX
QUESTION: What Did Gregor Mendel discover?

9th Grade Word of The Day

Use the dictionary to write the definition
and divide the words for each day
below into syllables.

○ MONDAY **WORD: *UNICYCLE***

EXAMPLE:

A unicycle is a vehicle that touches the ground
with only one wheel.

u-ni-cy-cle

TUESDAY WORD: acquaintance

WEDNESDAY WORD: actuality

THURSDAY WORD: diurnal

FRIDAY WORD: poignant

SATURDAY / SUNDAY WORD: maneuver

Write Words In ABC Order

_____

_____

_____

_____

_____

_____

For each word, find one synonym & one
antonym. (if none: write word + none)

_____

_____

_____

_____

_____

_____

_____

_____

_____

_____

_____

_____

9th Grade Word of The Day

Use the dictionary to write the definition
and divide the words for each day
below into syllables.

○ MONDAY WORD: *UNICYCLE*

EXAMPLE:

A unicycle is a vehicle that touches the ground
with only one wheel.

u-ni-cy-cle

Write Words In ABC Order

TUESDAY WORD: renovate

WEDNESDAY WORD: situated

**For each word, find one synonym & one
antonym.** (if none: write word + none)

THURSDAY WORD: impasse

FRIDAY WORD: mischievous

SATURDAY / SUNDAY WORD: distinction

9th Grade Word of The Day

Use the dictionary to write the definition
and divide the words for each day
below into syllables.

○ MONDAY WORD: *UNICYCLE*

EXAMPLE:

A unicycle is a vehicle that touches the ground
with only one wheel.

u-ni-cy-cle

Write Words In ABC Order

_____

_____

_____

_____

_____

_____

TUESDAY WORD: labyrinth

WEDNESDAY WORD: embroidery

**For each word, find one synonym & one
antonym.** (if none: write word + none)

_____

THURSDAY WORD: pittance

_____

_____

_____

FRIDAY WORD: insufficient

_____

_____

_____

_____

_____

SATURDAY / SUNDAY WORD: idiopathic

_____

_____

_____

_____

9th Grade Word of The Day

Use the dictionary to write the definition
and divide the words for each day
below into syllables.

○ MONDAY WORD: *UNICYCLE*

EXAMPLE:

A unicycle is a vehicle that touches the ground
with only one wheel.

u-ni-cy-cle

TUESDAY WORD: facsimile

WEDNESDAY WORD: subtle

THURSDAY WORD: prominent

FRIDAY WORD: scorned

SATURDAY / SUNDAY WORD: luxurious

Write Words In ABC Order

_____

_____

_____

_____

_____

_____

For each word, find one synonym & one
antonym. (if none: write word + none)

_____

_____

_____

_____

_____

_____

_____

_____

_____

_____

_____

_____

_____

9th Grade Biology: Heredity

Have you ever wondered why your grandmother believes your eyes are similar to your mother's or that you have your father's athletic abilities? Have you ever wondered why some people say "like father, like son"?

A trait is a distinguishing quality of a person, such as his personality or physical appearance. Your teacher might state that you have a shyness trait.

Traits are qualities that we acquire from our parents. Your shyness could have sprung from the fact that your mother was shy when she was your age.

If both of your parents are allergic to peanuts, you likely will be allergic to them as well. Heredity is defined as the transmission of mental and physical characteristics from one generation to the next.

Parents with black hair, for example, are more likely to have children with black hair, just as parents who are tall are more likely to have tall children.

The basic units of heredity are genes. They are made up of DNA and are a part of the chromosome, which is a more prominent structure. Genes include information that determines the qualities an organism inherits from its parents. They determine characteristics such as hair color, height, and eye color.

Multiple Choice (2 points each)

1. **Genes are located in the _____ of cells.**
   a. Chromosomes
   b. Polydactyl cats.
   c. Binary fission

2. **Genes control specific _____ which determine which traits are expressed.**
   a. Binary fission
   b. Proteins
   c. Fragmentation

3. **Mutations in genes can result in changes in proteins.**
   a. True
   b. False

4. **One example of a genetic mutation is _____.**
   a. Polydactyl cats.
   b. Parthenogenesis
   c. Fragmentation

5. **Which is a representation of "variance of traits"?**
   a. Humans creating offspring through sexual reproduction.
   b. Chromosomes
   c. Regeneration

6. **Humans have two alleles for each trait, one from each _____.**
   a. Chromosomes
   b. Parent.
   c. Polydactyl cats.

7. **Mutations can be beneficial, harmful, or neutral**
   a. True
   b. False

8. **What is a karyotype?**
   a. Regeneration
   b. A chart that shows chromosome pairs.
   c. Polydactyl cats.

9. **Asexual reproduction produces offspring that are genetically _____ to the parent.**
   a. Parent.
   b. Chromosomes
   c. Identical

10. **A form of asexual reproduction where an organism is split into fragments is called**
    a. Fragmentation
    b. Parthenogenesis
    c. Regeneration

11. **Bacteria reproduce through a process called...**
    a. A chart that shows chromosome pairs.
    b. Deoxyribonucleic Acid
    c. Binary fission

12. **Worms reproduce through a process called...**
    a. Regeneration
    b. Fragmentation
    c. Parthenogenesis

13. **A specialized form of asexual reproduction where an organism can replace a lost or injured part of it's body is called...**
    a. Fragmentation
    b. Parthenogenesis
    c. Regeneration

14. **A type of asexual reproduction where an organism can be produced from unfertilized eggs is called ...**
    a. Fragmentation
    b. Parthenogenesis
    c. Regeneration

15. **A punnett square represents both the genotype and the phenotype of an organism.**
    a. True
    b. False

16. **The capital letter in a genotype represents the recessive traits of an organism.**
    a. True
    b. False

17. **A phenotype represents the _____ characteristics of an organism.**
    a. Parent.
    b. Physical
    c. Parthenogenesis

18. **DNA stands for _____.**
    a. Deoxyribonucleic Acid
    b. Regeneration
    c. Parent.

19. **CRISPR is a gene-editing tool that uses a family of DNA sequences that are found in bacteria.**
    a. True
    b. False

20. **A punnett square has four boxes: Rr, RR, Rr, rr. What is the probability that the parents with have offspring with recessive traits?**
    a. 25%
    b. Humans creating offspring through sexual reproduction.
    c. Parthenogenesis

9th Grade Math:Test Your Knowledge Refresher

1. Addends are numbers_____

    a. used in an addition problem.

    b. used in an addition or multiplication problem.

    c. used in an subtraction problem.

2. What is an example of an Addend?

    a. In $9 + 1 = 10$, the 9 and the 10 are addends.

    b. In $8 - 3 = 5$, the 8 and the 3 are addends.

    c. In $8 + 3 = 11$, the 8 and the 3 are addends.

3. What is a fact family?

    a. a group of math facts or equations created using the same set of numbers.

    b. is when you take one number and add it together a number of times.

    c. is taking away one or more items from a group of items.

4. Which is an example of a fact family?

    a. 2, 4, and 6: $2 \times 2 = 4$, $4 \times 2 = 8$, $6 - 2 = 4$, and $6 - 4 = 2$.

    b. 1, 2, and 12: $1 + 1 = 2$, $2 + 2 = 4$, $12 - 12 = 0$, and $12 - 2 = 10$.

    c. 10, 2, and 12: $10 + 2 = 12$, $2 + 10 = 12$, $12 - 10 = 2$, and $12 - 2 = 10$.

5. The fact family for 3, 8 and 24 is a set of four multiplication and division facts. Which one is correct?

    a. $3 \times 8 = 24 | 8 \times 3 = 24 | 24 \div 3 = 8 | 24 \div 8 = 3$

    b. $3 + 8 = 11 | 8 \times 3 = 24 | 8 \div 8 = 0 | 24 \div 8 = 3$

    c. $3 \times 3 = 9 | 8 \times 3 = 24 | 24 + 3 = 27 | 24 \div 8 = 3$

6. A prime number is_____

    a. the ways that numbers are combined to make new numbers.

    b. any number that is only divisible by itself and 1.

    c. the number you are rounding followed by 5, 6, 7, 8, or 9.

7. Examples of prime numbers_____

    a. 2, 8 and 15

    b. 2, 5 and 17

    c. 4, 6 and 10

8. Numbers such as _____ are not prime, because they are divisible by more than just themselves and 1.

    a. 2 or 7

    b. 5 or 11

    c. 15 or 21

9. Prime factor is the factor_____

    a. of the first number which is NOT a prime number.

    b. of the smallest to greatest prime number starting with 0..

    c. of the given number which is a prime number.

10. The prime factors of 15 _____

    a. are 3 and 5 (because 3×5=15, and 3 and 5 are prime numbers)

    b. are 5 and 10 (because 5+10=15, and 10 and 5 are prime numbers)

    c. are 25 and 10 (because 25-10=15, and 10 and 5 are prime numbers)

11. A factor tree is a _____

    a. natural numbers greater than one that are not products of two smaller natural numbers.

    b. diagram that is used to break down a number into its factors until all the numbers left are prime.

    c. is divisible by 1, and it's divisible by itself.

12. The greatest common denominator is the _____

    a. smallest positive integer that multiplies the numbers without a remainder.

    b. largest negative integer that subtracts the numbers without a remainder.

    c. largest positive integer that divides the numbers without a remainder.

13. The greatest common factor of 8 and 12 is_____?

    a. 12

    b. 6

    c. 4

14. The lowest common denominator is the _____?

    a. lowest common multiple of the denominators of a set of fractions.

    b. lowest common multiple of the denominators of a group of numbers divided by 10.

    c. lowest common subtraction of the first number of a set of fractions.

15. What is the LCD of 12 and 8?

    a. 12 and 8 is 24

    b. 12 and 8 is 32

    c. 12 and 8 is 20

16. This math concept tells you that to divide means to split fairly.

    a. Division

    b. Addition

    c. Algebra

17. Reduce 48/28 to lowest terms.

    a. 12/5

    b. 12/7

    c. 7/28

18. Which of the following fractions CANNOT be reduced further?

    a. 5/3

    b. 33/12

    c. 16/9

19. It is possible to make a fraction simpler without completely simplifying it.

    a. True

    b. False

20. Factor 18 into prime factors:

    a. 18 = 3 * 3 * 2

    b. 18 = 2 * 3 * 3

    c. 18 = 1 * 3 * 2

21. An improper fraction is one where the numerator is smaller than the denominator.

    a. True

    b. False

22. Fractions that have a numerator with a higher value than the denominator

    a. simple fractions

    b. simplified fractions

    c. improper fractions

9th Grade Reading Comprehension: Social Media Safety

1. In the last 20 years, socializing has evolved dramatically. __Interactions__ between people are referred to as socializing.
2. It now frequently refers to accessing the Internet via social media or websites that allow you to __connect__ and interact with other people.
3. Ascertain that your computer is outfitted with up-to-date computer __security__ software.
4. This software detects and removes __viruses__ that are harmful to your computer.
5. When you use your computer, these viruses can sometimes hack into it and __steal__ your information, such as __logins__ .
6. Create strong __passwords__ for all of your social media accounts.
7. These can be as loose or as __restrictive__ as you want them to be.
8. This enables your computer to block __pop-ups__ and warn you when you are about to visit a potentially harmful website.
9. - Don't __post__ anything you wouldn't want broadcast to the entire world.
10. __Personal__ information about one's identity should not be posted or shared on social media.
11. This information can be used to recreate your __identity__ and should never be made public.
12. Make use of the __privacy__ settings on the social media website.
13. Be cautious about what you post on any social media __platform__ .
14. Posting something __negative__ about someone hurts their character and opens the door for them, or someone else, to do the same to you.
15. If you are not in a good mood or are upset, think twice.
16. What you post could be __harmful__ to you or someone else.
17. If you are in a bad social media __relationship__ and are being harassed or bullied, you can report it to the social media company.
18. They all have __policies__ in place to deal with people who __abuse__ their websites.
19. Make a note of these __incidents__ and report them to the company. You may also save the life of another person.

9th Grade Science: Different Blood Types

compatible	transfusion	recipient's	antibodies	survive
donate	bloodstream	eight	negative	antigens

What comes to mind when you think of blood? It may be the color red, a hospital, or even a horror film! Blood is something that your body requires to __survive__, regardless of how you feel about it. Did you realize, though, that not everyone has the same blood type? There are __eight__ different kinds in total! The letters A, B, and O, as well as positive or __negative__ signs, distinguish these blood types. O+, O-, A+, A-, B+, B-, AB+, and AB- are the eight blood types.

What Is the Importance of Blood Types?

Don't be concerned if your blood type differs from that of others! There is no such thing as a better or healthier blood type. The sole reason to know your blood type is in case you need to __donate__ or give blood to someone in an emergency. A blood __transfusion__ is a process of transferring blood from one person to another.

Blood transfusions are only effective when the donor's blood is __compatible__ with the __recipient's__ blood. Some blood types don't mix well because the body produces antibodies to fight off any unfamiliar __antigens__ that enter the __bloodstream__. Antibodies act as warriors in your blood, guarding you against alien intruders. Assume you have Type A blood, which contains A antigens solely, and someone with Type B blood wishes to donate blood to you. Your body does not recognize B antigens; thus, __antibodies__ are produced to combat them! This has the potential to make you sick. As a result, people with Type A blood should only receive blood from those with Type A blood or Type O blood, as O blood lacks both A and B antigens.

9th Grade Math: Look It Up! Pop Quiz

Learn some basic vocabulary words that you will come across again and again in the course of your studies in algebra. By knowing the definitions of most algebra words, you will be able to construct and solve algebra problems much more easily.

Find the answer to the questions below by *looking up each word. (The wording can be tricky. Take your time.)*

1. improper fraction
   a. a fraction that represents both positive and negative numbers that has a value more than 1
   b. a fraction in which the numerator is greater than the denominator, is always 1 or greater
   c. a fraction that the denominator is equal to the numerator

2. equivalent fraction
   a. a fraction that has a DIFFERENT value as a given fraction
   b. a fraction that has the SAME value as a given fraction
   c. a fraction that has an EQUAL value as a given fraction

3. simplest form of fraction
   a. an equivalent fraction for which the only common factor of the numerator and denominator is 1
   b. an equivalent fraction for which the only least factor of the denominator is -1
   c. an equal value fraction for which the only common factor of the numerator and denominator is -1

4. mixed number
   a. the sum of a positive fraction and a reciprocal
   b. the sum of a whole number and a proper fraction
   c. the sum of a variable and a fraction

5. reciprocal
   a. a number that can be multiplied by another number to make 1
   b. a number that can be divided by another number to make 10
   c. a number that can be subtracted by another number to make -1

6. percent
   a. a ratio that compares a number to 100
   b. a percentage that compares a number to 0.1
   c. a 1/2 ratio that equals a number to 100

7. sequence

    a. a set of addition numbers that follow a operation

    b. a set of letters & numbers divided by 5 that makes a sequence

    c. a set of numbers that follow a pattern

8. arithmetic sequence

    a. a sequence where ONE term is found by dividing or subtracting the exact same number to the previous term

    b. a sequence where NO term is found by multiplying the exact same number to the previous term

    c. a sequence where EACH term is found by adding or subtracting the exact same number to the previous term

9. geometric sequence

    a. a sequence where each term is found by multiplying or dividing by the exact same number to the previous term

    b. a sequence where each term is divided or subtracted by the same fraction to the previous term

    c. a sequence where each term is solved by adding or dividing by a different number to the previous term

10. order of operations

    a. the procedure to follow when simplifying a numerical expression

    b. the procedure to follow when adding any fraction by 100

    c. the procedure to follow when simplifying an equation with the same answer

11. variable expression

    a. a mathematical phrase that contains numbers and operation symbols

    b. a mathematical phrase that contains variables, addition, and operation sequence

    c. a mathematical phrase that contains variables, numbers, and operation symbols

12. absolute value

    a. a whole number on the number line from one to zero

    b. the distance a number is from zero on the number line

    c. the range a number is from one on the number line

13. integers

    a. a set of numbers that equal to fractions line variables

    b. a set of numbers that includes equal numbers and their difference

    c. a set of numbers that includes whole numbers and their opposites

14. x-axis

    a. the horizontal number line that, together with the y-axis, establishes the coordinate plane

    b. the vertical number line that, together with the y-axis, establishes the coordinate plane

    c. both horizontal & vertical number line that, together with the y-axis, establishes the coordinate plane

15. y-axis

    a. the horizontal number line that, together with the x-axis, establishes the coordinate plane

    b. the vertical number line that, together with the x-axis, establishes the coordinate plane

    c. the vertical number line that, together with the x or y-axis, establishes the coordinate plane

16. coordinate plane

    a. plane formed by two number lines (the horizontal x-axis and the vertical y-axis) intersecting at their zero points

    b. plane formed by three number line (the vertical y-axis and the horizontal x-axis) intersecting at their two points

    c. plane formed by one number line (the horizontal y-axis and the vertical x-axis) intersecting at their -1 points

17. quadrant

    a. three sections on the axis plane formed by the intersection of the x-axis and the y-axis

    b. one of four sections on the coordinate plane formed by the intersection of the x-axis and the y-axis

    c. one of two sections on the four plane formed by the intersection of the x-axis

18. ordered pair

    a. a pair of integer number sets that gives the range of a point in the axis plane. Also known as the "x-axis" of a point.

    b. a pair of equal numbers that gives the range of a point in the axis plane. Also known as the "y-axis" of a point.

    c. a pair of numbers that gives the location of a point in the coordinate plane. Also known as the "coordinates" of a point.

19. x-coordinate

    a. the number that indicates the position of a point to the left or right of the y-axis

    b. the number that indicates the range of a point to the left ONLY of the y-axis

    c. the number that indicates the range of a point to both sides of the x-axis

20. y-coordinate

    a. the number that indicates the value of a point only above the x-axis

    b. the number that indicates the position of a point above or below the x-axis

    c. the number that indicates the value or range of a point only above the y-axis

21. inverse operations

    a. operations that divide evenly into each other

    b. operations that undo each other

    c. operations that equals to each other

22. inequality

    a. a math sentence that uses a symbol (<, >, ≤, ≥, ≠) to indicate that the left and right sides of the sentence hold values that are different

    b. a math sentence that uses a letter (x or y) to indicate that the left and right sides of the sentence hold values that are different

    c. a math sentence that uses both numbers and letters (1=x or 2=y) to indicate that the left and right sides of the sentence hold values that are different

23. perimeter

    a. the range around the outside or inside of a figure

    b. the distance around the outside of a figure

    c. the distance around the inside of a figure

24. circumference

    a. the distance around a circle

    b. the cube squared value around a circle

    c. the range around a square

25. area

    a. the number of circle units inside a 3-dimensional figure

    b. the number of triangle units inside a 2-dimensional figure

    c. | the number of square units inside a 2-dimensional figure |

26. volume

    a. the number of cubic squared units inside a 2-dimensional figure

    b. the number of cubic or circle units inside a 1-dimensional figure

    c. | the number of cubic units inside a 3-dimensional figure |

27. radius

    a. | a line segment that runs from the center of the circle to somewhere on the circle |

    b. a line segment that runs from the middle of the circle to end of the circle

    c. a line segment that runs from the middle of the square to start of the square

28. chord

    a. a circle distance that runs from somewhere on the far left to another place on the circle

    b. a line around a circle that runs from somewhere on the right to another place on the circle

    c. | a line segment that runs from somewhere on the circle to another place on the circle |

29. diameter

    a. a thin line that passes through the end of the circle

    b. a 1/2" line that passes through the top of the circle

    c. | a chord that passes through the center of the circle |

30. mean

    a. the sum of the data items added by the number of data items minus 2

    b. | the sum of the data items divided by the number of data items |

    c. the sum of the data items divdied by the number of even data items less than 1

31. median

    a. | the middle data item found after sorting the data items in ascending order |

    b. the first data item found after sorting the data items in descending order

    c. the middle & last data item found after sorting the data items in ascending order

32. mode

    a. the data item that occurs less than two times

    b. the data item that occurs when two or more numbers equal

    c. | the data item that occurs most often |

33. range

    a. | the difference between the highest and the lowest data item |

    b. the difference between the numbers less than 10 and the lowest number item 2

    c. the difference between the middle number and the lowest number item

34. outlier

    a. | a data item that is much higher or much lower than all the other data items |

    b. a data item that is much lower or less than all the other data items

    c. a data item that is always higher than 1 or less than all the other data items

35. ratio

    a. a comparison of two quantities by subtraction

    b. a comparison of two quantities by multiplication

    c. | a comparison of two quantities by division |

36. rate

    a. a ratio that has equal range and distance measured within the first unit set

    b. a ratio that has equal quantities measured in the same units

    c. | a ratio that compares quantities measured in different units |

37. proportion

    a. | a statement (equation) showing two ratios to be equal |

    b. a statement (property) showing the distance between two variables

    c. a statement (ratio) showing five or more ratios to be equal

38. outcomes

    a. possible answer when two numbers are the same

    b. possible results when the action is by division

    c. | possible results of action |

39. probability

    a. a ratio that explains the likelihood of two division problems with equal answers

    b. | a ratio that explains the likelihood of an event |

    c. a ratio that explains the likelihood of the distance and miles between to places

40. theoretical probability

    a. the probability of the highest favorable number of possible outcomes (based on what is not expected to occur).

    b. | the ratio of the number of favorable outcomes to the number of possible outcomes (based on what is expected to occur). |

    c. the probability of the lowest favorable number of possible outcomes (based on what is expected to occur when added by 5).

41. experimental probability

    a. the ratio of the number of times multiplied by the number of events that occur to the number of events times 5 (based on real experimental data).

    b. the ratio of the number of times by 2 when an event occurs to the number of times times 2 an experiment is done (based on real experimental data).

    c. | the ratio of the number of times an event occurs to the number of times an experiment is done (based on real experimental data). |

42. distributive property

    a. | a way to simplify an expression that contains a single term being multiplied by a group of terms. |

    b. a way to simplify an expression that contains a range of like terms being divided by a group of like terms.

    c. a way to simplify an expression that contains a equal like term being added by a group of terms.

43. term

    a. a number, a variable, or probability of an equal number and a variable(s)

    b. a number, a variable, or expression of a range of numbers and a variable(s)

    c. a number, a variable, or product of a number and a variable(s)

44. Constant

    a. a term with no variable + y part (i.e. 4+y)

    b. a term with no variable - x value (i.e. 8-x)

    c. a term with no variable part (i.e. a number)

45. Coefficient

    a. a number that multiplies a variable

    b. a number that divides a variable

    c. a number that subtracts a variable

46. Probability is the likelihood of something happening.

    a. True

    b. False

47. To calculate probability, you need to know how many possible options or _____ there are and how many right combinations you have.

    a. outcomes

    b. numbers

    c. fraction

48. _, _, and _ have two common factors: 2 and 4.

    a. 2, 6, and 9

    b. 12, 20, and 24

    c. 1,4, and 24

49. How do you write a polynomial expression?

    a. 3x2 -2x-10

    b. 32 -2x-+10y

    c. y+3x2 -2x-10

50. How can you simplify rational expression?

    a. eliminate all factors that are common of the numerator and the denominator

    b. eliminate only 1 factor that are common of the numerator and the denominator

    c. eliminate NO factors that are common of the numerator and the denominator

51. The slope intercept form is one of many forms that represents the linear relationship between two variables.

    a. True

    b. False

52. The slope intercept form equation is written as follows:

    a. $z = a x + b$

    b. $y = y x + m$

    c. $y = m x + b$

53. Simplifying radicals is that we do NOT remove the radicals from the denominator.

    a. True

    b. False

54. 2 1/3 is a mixed fraction.

    a. True

    b. False

55. The word _____ literally means 'per hundred.' We use this symbol - %.

    a. asterisk

    b. percent

    c. divide

56. less than or equal to symbol

    a. $\leq$

    b. $<$

    c. $\geq$

57. distance between points x and y

    a. $|x-y|$

    b. $|x+y|$

    c. $|x-y+x+y|$

58. greater than or equal to

    a. $<$

    b. $\leq$

    c. $\geq$

Order of Operations

1) $(50 - 2) \div 3 - 7^2$
$48 \quad \div 3 - 7^2$
$48 \quad \div 3 - 49$
$\qquad 16 - 49$
$\qquad -33$

2) $3 \times (11 + 6) - 5^2$
$3 \times \quad 17 \quad - 5^2$
$3 \times \quad 17 \quad - 25$
$51 \qquad - 25$
$\qquad 26$

3) $(28 - 2^2) \div (1 + 5)$
$(28 - 4) \div (1 + 5)$
$24 \qquad \div \qquad 6$
$\qquad 4$

4) $(5 \times 4 - 7^2) + 3$
$(5 \times 4 - 49) + 3$
$(\quad 20 - 49) + 3$
$\qquad -29 \qquad + 3$
$\qquad -26$

5) $(13 \times 6 + 7^2) + 4$
$(13 \times 6 + 49) + 4$
$(\quad 78 + 49) + 4$
$\qquad 127 \qquad + 4$
$\qquad 131$

6) $(12 - 5)^2 + (20 \div 2)$
$7^2 \qquad + \qquad 10$
$49 \qquad + \qquad 10$
$\qquad 59$

7) $(44 - 2^2) \div (4 + 4)$
$(44 - 4) \div (4 + 4)$
$40 \qquad \div \qquad 8$
$\qquad 5$

8) $5 \times (9 + 2) - 5^2$
$5 \times \quad 11 \quad - 5^2$
$5 \times \quad 11 \quad - 25$
$55 \qquad - 25$
$\qquad 30$

9) $(44 - 4) \div 8 + 5^2$
$40 \quad \div 8 + 5^2$
$40 \quad \div 8 + 25$
$\qquad 5 + 25$
$\qquad 30$

10) $(14 - 5)^2 + (8 \div 4)$
$9^2 \qquad + \qquad 2$
$81 \qquad + \qquad 2$
$\qquad 83$

ANSWERS

Quadrant Order

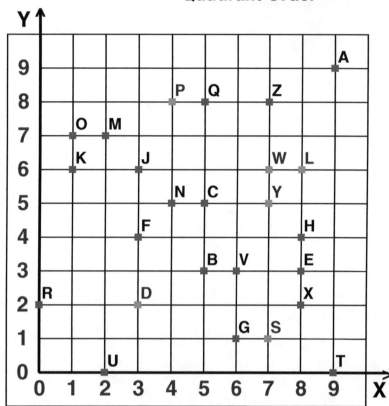

Tell what point is located at each ordered pair.

1) (8,3) __E__   6) (1,6) __K__

2) (9,9) __A__   7) (4,5) __N__

3) (8,2) __X__   8) (0,2) __R__

4) (6,3) __V__   9) (9,0) __T__

5) (6,1) __G__   10) (5,8) __Q__

Write the ordered pair for each given point.

11) **B** (5,3)   14) **Z** (7,8)   17) **O** (1,7)

12) **M** (2,7)   15) **J** (3,6)   18) **U** (2,0)

13) **C** (5,5)   16) **H** (8,4)   19) **F** (3,4)

Plot the following points on the coorinate grid.

20) **W** (7,6)   22) **L** (8,6)   24) **Y** (7,5)

21) **S** (7,1)   23) **D** (3,2)   25) **P** (4,8)

9th Grade Spelling Words
Unscramble

symphony	analysis	agriculture	twelfth	abundant	tendency
souvenir	technique	laborious	ambassador	sophomore	specific
symbol	specimen	aggressive	jealousy	absorption	journal
island	acceptable	syllable	absence	amateur	temperature

1. NECASEB   a b s e n c e

2. PNSOABROTI   a b s o r p t i o n

3. ABDNUTNA   a b u n d a n t

4. BLEATAPCEC   a c c e p t a b l e

5. SLYBLELA   s y l l a b l e

6. BLOMYS   s y m b o l

7. OMHYPSYN   s y m p h o n y

8. ENUTICQHE   t e c h n i q u e

9. EPTMERUATRE   t e m p e r a t u r e

10. EYNNDCET   t e n d e n c y

11. GEEGSARVIS   a g g r e s s i v e

12. ARTEULICRUG   a g r i c u l t u r e

13. UMTEAAR   a m a t e u r

14. AASBOARMSD   a m b a s s a d o r

15. LISASNAY   a n a l y s i s

16. PMREHSOOO   s o p h o m o r e

17. VOESINUR   s o u v e n i r

18. CSPFCIEI   s p e c i f i c

19. SPCMENEI   s p e c i m e n

20. DSLINA   i s l a n d

21. JSULYEOA   j e a l o u s y

22. JRUOLNA   j o u r n a l

23. ASILOBURO   l a b o r i o u s

24. TELWTHF   t w e l f t h

9th Grade Spelling Words Crossword

Across

1. We will meet at our summer ___ for the wedding
3. My father studied _____.
6. The _____ of the donors came as a surprise.
7. There was a growing ____ between the two sides.
8. The old home was in a _____ state.
9. The ____ between the villages was growing larger.

Down

2. The lamb ____ is nearly done cooking
4. The economic ____ appears to be working.
5. I've always wanted to play the _____.
10. The people were ____ of his motives.
11. Pass the ____ to me so that I can take my medicine.
12. The doctor told my grandma to take only one ____ a day.

VITAMIN RESIDENCE
ANIMOSITY WARY
XYLOPHONE SHANK
CHASM PODIATRY
SYRINGE GENEROSITY
STIMULUS RUINOUS

9th Grade Health: Check Your Symptoms

1. **I've got a pain in my head.**
   - a. Stiff neck
   - b. headache

2. **I was out in the sun too long.**
   - a. Sunburn
   - b. Fever

3. **I've got a small itchy lump or bump.**
   - a. Rash
   - b. Insect bite

4. **I might be having a heart attack.**
   - a. Cramps
   - b. Chest pain

5. **I've lost my voice.**
   - a. Laryngitis
   - b. Sore throat

6. **I need to blow my nose a lot.**
   - a. Runny nose
   - b. Blood Nose

7. **I have an allergy. I have a**
   - a. Rash
   - b. Insect bite

8. **My shoe rubbed my heel. I have a**
   - a. Rash
   - b. Blister

9. **The doctor gave me antibiotics. I have a/an**
   - a. Infection
   - b. Cold

10. **I think I want to vomit. I am**
    - a. Nauseous
    - b. Bloated

11. **My arm is not broken. It is**
    - a. Scratched
    - b. Sprained

12. **My arm touched the hot stove. It is**
    - a. Burned
    - b. Bleeding

13. **I have an upset stomach. I might**
    - a. Cough
    - b. Vomit

14. **The doctor put plaster on my arm. It is**
    - a. Sprained
    - b. Broken

15. **If you cut your finger it will**
    - a. Burn
    - b. Bleed

16. **I hit my hip on a desk. It will**
    - a. Burn
    - b. Bruise

17. **When you have hay-fever you will**
    - a. Sneeze
    - b. Wheeze

18. **A sharp knife will**
    - a. Scratch
    - b. Cut

9th Grade Grammar: some, any, a, an

A is used when the next word starts with a consonant sound.
AN is used when the next word starts with a vowel sound.
Some is generally used in positive sentences.
Any is generally used in negative sentences.

Rewrite the *scrambled words* so they form a complete *sentence*.

1. We don't have any apples.
   We   any   have   don't   apples.

2. We can make some sandwiches for lunch.
   make   some   lunch.   for   sandwiches   We   can

3. There isn't any milk in the fridge.
   fridge.   in   There   the   isn't   any   milk

4. I need to buy an onion and some tomatoes.
   buy   I   to   tomatoes.   and   an   onion   need   some

5. She doesn't need any tomatoes or carrots.
   carrots.   need   any   tomatoes   or   doesn't   She

6. Do we have any potatoes?
   have   any   we   potatoes?   Do

7. We have some strawberries but we don't have any grapes.
   some   grapes.   We   have   don't   but   we   strawberries   any   have

8. There isn't any sugar in the bowl.
   There   any   isn't   sugar   in   bowl.   the

9. Can I have a banana, please?
   Can   a   I   banana,   have   please?

10. Are there any apples on the counter? _____

on · there · the · any · apples · counter? · Are

11. It wasn't an easy decision. _____

decision. · an · wasn't · easy · It

12. She forced a smile. _____

a · She · forced · smile.

13. I have an appointment. _____

an · I · appointment. · have

14. He is an excellent horseman, you know. _____

horseman, · you · excellent · He · an · is · know.

15. It's an easy job, like I expected. _____

I · job, · an · easy · It's · expected. · like

16. That was a no-brainer. _____

That · was · no-brainer. · a

17. I think you owe me an explanation. _____

I · an · owe · me · think · you · explanation.

18. Suddenly he stopped at the foot of a tree. _____

at · the · tree. · foot · of · he · stopped · a · Suddenly

9th Grade Grammar: Is vs. Are

Use **is** if the noun is singular. If the noun is plural or there are multiple nouns, use **are**.

1. _____ Billy?
    1. Where are
    2. Where's

2. _____ in the bed.
    1. They're
    2. He's

3. _____ Mum and Dad?
    1. Where's
    2. Where are

4. _____ in the kitchen.
    1. She's
    2. They're

5. _____ Grandpa?
    1. Where are
    2. Where's

6. _____ in the garden.
    1. He's
    2. She's

7. _____ Lucy and Lilly?
    1. Where's
    2. Where are

8. _____ in the park.
    1. She's
    2. They're

9. _____ my sister?
    1. Where are
    2. Where's

10. _____ in her bedroom.
    1. He's
    2. She's

11. _____ pupils?
    1. Where are
    2. Where's

12. _____ at school.
    1. He's
    2. They're

9th Grade Math Vocabulary Quiz

1. algebraic equation

equality of two expressions formulated by applying to a set of variables the algebraic operations

2. direct evidence

evidence that, if believed, directly proves a fact

3. variable

a symbol (usually a letter) standing in for an unknown numerical value in an equation

4. scale factor

the ratio of the lengths of two corresponding sides of two similar polygons or solids

5. computation

Finding an answer by using mathematics or logic

6. equivalent

two meanings, numbers, or quantities that are the same

7. equation

two math expressions are equal (indicated by the sign =)

8. analyze

to study or determine the nature and relationship of the parts of (something) by analysis

9. structure

the way that something is built, arranged, or organized

10. summarize

Express the most important facts or ideas about something or someone in a short and clear form

11. addends

A quantity to be added to another

12. place value

the basis of our entire number system

13. difference

The result of subtracting one number from another.

14. divisor

a number by which another number is to be divided.

15. numerator

number above the line of a fraction, showing the number of parts of the whole

16. quotient

number obtained by dividing one number by another

9th Grade Grammar: 8 Parts of Speech Matching

- NOUN. used to identify any of a class of people, places, or things
- PRONOUN. a word (such as I, he, she, you, it, we, or they) that is used instead of a noun or noun phrase
- VERB. a word used to describe an action, state, or occurrence
- ADJECTIVE. modify or describe a noun or a pronoun
- ADVERB. word that modifies (describes) a verb (she sings loudly), adverbs often end in -ly
- PREPOSITION. word or phrase that connects a noun or pronoun to a verb or adjective in a sentence
- CONJUNCTION. word used to join words, phrases, sentences, and clauses
- INTERJECTION. word or phrase that expresses something in a sudden or exclamatory way, especially an emotion

1	C	Identify the noun.	⇢	Lion
2	I	Identify the verb.	⇢	barked
3	F	What is an adjective?	⇢	a word that describes nouns and pronouns
4	B	Three sets of nouns	⇢	mother, truck, banana
5	E	Three sets of adverbs	⇢	always, beautifully, often
6	G, H	above, across, against	⇢	preposition
7	D	but, and, because, although	⇢	conjunctions
8	J	Wow! Ouch! Hurrah!	⇢	Interjection
9	A	Mary and Joe are friends.	⇢	verb
10	G, H	Jane ran <u>around</u> the corner yesterday.	⇢	preposition

[Student worksheet has a 4 line writing exercise here.]

9th Grade Grammar:
Subjunctive Mood

Wishes, proposals, ideas, imagined circumstances, and assertions that are not true are all expressed in the subjunctive mood. The subjunctive is frequently used to indicate an action that a person hopes or wishes to be able to undertake now or in the future. In general, a verb in the subjunctive mood denotes a scenario or state that is a possibility, hope, or want. It expresses a conditional, speculative, or hypothetical sense of a verb.

When verbs of advice or suggestion are used, the subjunctive mood is utilized. After verbs of recommendation or advice, the subjunctive appears in a phrase beginning with the word -that.

Here are a few verbs that are commonly used in the subjunctive mood to recommend or advise.

- advise, ask, demand, prefer

1. Writers use the subjunctive mood to express _____ or _____ conditions.

   a. imaginary or hoped-for

   b.

2. Which is NOT a common marker of the subjunctive mood?

   a.

   b. memories

3. Which is NOT an example of a hope-for verb?

   a. demand

   b. need

4. Subjunctive mood is used to show a situation is not _____.

   a. fictional or fabricated

   b. entirely factual or certain

5. Which of the below statements is written in the subjunctive mood?

   a. I wish I were a millionaire.

   b. What would you do with a million dollars?

6. The indicative mood is used to state facts and opinions, as in:

   a. My mom's fried chicken is my favorite food in the world.

   b. Smells, taste, chew

7. The imperative mood is used to give commands, orders, and instructions, as in:

   a. Eat your salad.

   b. I love salad!

8. The interrogative mood is used to ask a question, as in:

   a. Have you eaten all of your pizza yet?

   b. I ordered 2 slices of pizza.

9. The conditional mood uses the conjunction "if" or "when" to express a condition and its result, as in:

   a. Blue is my favorite color, so I paint with it often.

   b. If I eat too much lasagna, I'll have a stomach ache later.

10. The subjunctive mood is used to express wishes, proposals, suggestions, or imagined situations, as in:

   a. Yesterday was Monday, and I ate pizza.

   b. I prefer that my mom make pasta rather than tuna.

9th Grade Grammar: Linking Verbs

A linking verb links the topic of a phrase to a word that describes the subject, such as a condition or a relationship. They don't depict any action; instead, they serve to connect the subject to the rest of the phrase or sentence.

In a sentence, helping verbs always appear before the primary verb. They complete the structure of a phrase by adding information to the main verb. They can also help you understand how time is expressed in a sentence.

To connect nouns, pronouns, and adjectives, both the supporting and linking verb are utilized.

1. Which of the following examples best shows what a linking verb is?

   a. Shows action

   b. Connects a subject to the predicate

   c. Connects a noun and verb

2. How can you determine the difference between a helping verb and a linking verb?

   a. There is no difference between a helping verb and a linking verb.

   b. The helping verb is combined with an action verb.

   c. The helping verb or adverb shows action.

3. Which words belong to the category of state of being verbs?

   a. were, am, are, been

   b. flow, jump, bounce

   c. she, he, they, did

4. Which of the following examples does not connect subject and a predicate?

   a. Tiffany is an awesome student.

   b. She became the best mom ever!

   c. It danced quietly and smoothly.

5. What distinguishes a connecting verb from an action verb?

   a. It is an adjective.

   b. It shows no action.

   c. It shows action and no action.

6. The tomato smells rotten. Which is the linking verb in this sentence?

   a. rotten

   b. smells

   c. tomato

7. My brother is mad when he's hungry.

   a. is

   b. mad

   c. when

8. Identify the linking verb: The girl was frightened.

   a. girl

   b. was

   c. frightened

9. What is the linking verb in the sentence? Rob and Tony were class leaders.

   a. were

   b. class

   c. none

10. The Queen_____ busy laying eggs.

   a. is

   b. bee

   c. are

9th Grade Science: Space

No one can hear you scream in space. This is due to the fact that space is devoid of air - it is a vacuum. In a vacuum, sound waves cannot travel. 'Outer space' begins roughly 100 kilometers above the Earth's surface, where the atmosphere that surrounds our planet dissipates. Space appears as a black blanket speckled with stars because there is no air to disperse sunlight and generate a blue sky.

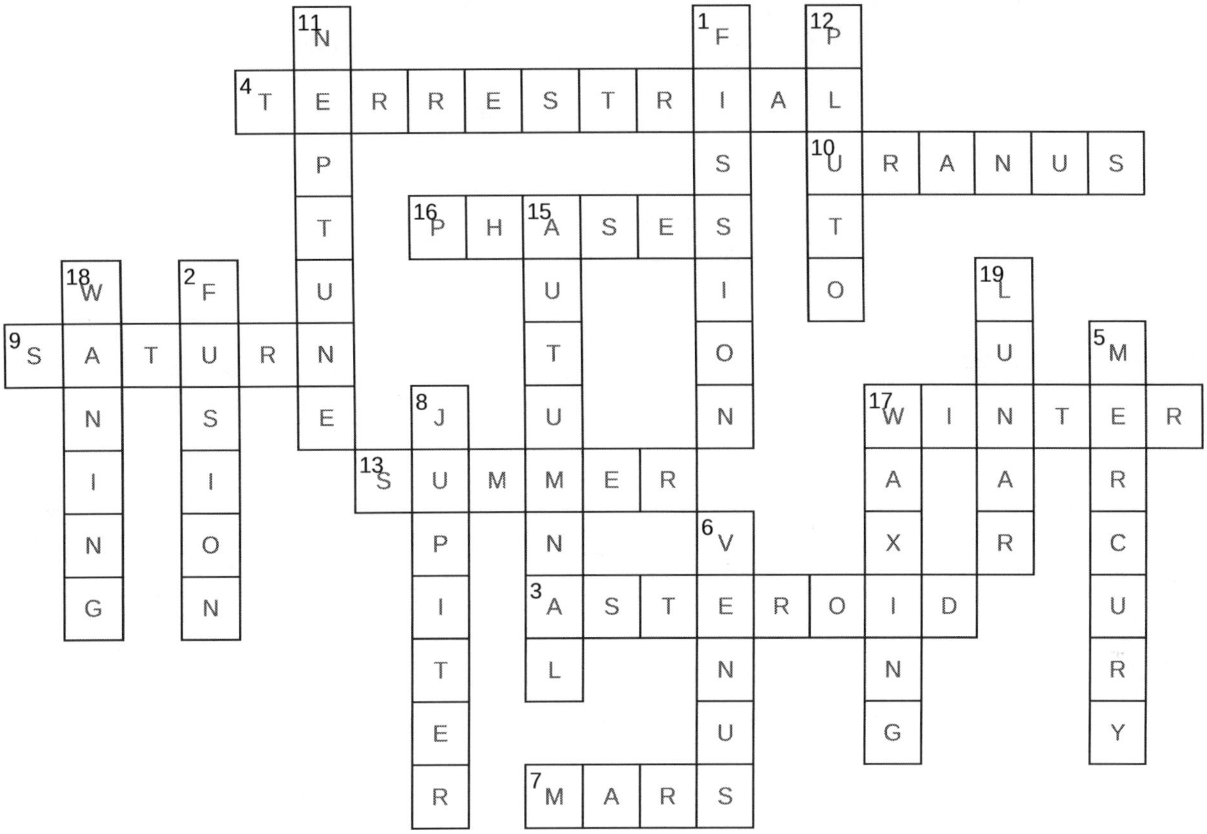

[Crossword puzzle grid with answers:]

- 4 Across: TERRESTRIAL
- 10 Across: URANUS
- 16 Across: PHASES
- 9 Across: SATURN
- 17 Across: WINTER
- 13 Across: SUMMER
- 3 Across: ASTEROID
- 7 Across: MARS
- 11 Down: NEPTUNE
- 1 Down: FISSION
- 12 Down: PLUTO
- 18 Down: WANING
- 2 Down: FUSION
- 19 Down: LUNAR
- 5 Down: MERCURY
- 8 Down: JUPITER
- 6 Down: VENUS
- 15 Down: AUTUMN
- 17 Down: WAXING

Across

3. The 4 inner planets and 4 outer planets are separated by the _____ Belt.
4. The 4 inner planets are referred to as _____ planets because they are rocky and dense- Earth like
7. only about 1/2 the size of earth- tilted similar to earth- rusty surface- 2 moons
9. Revolves as rapidly as Jupiter- second largest planet- could float in water- Oh yeah...it has rings
10. Sideways rotation- retrograde rotation- has 11 very thin rings
13. _____ Solstice is when we have the longest amount of daylight for that year and the shortest night
16. The way we see the moon as it orbits around the sun and reflects the Sun's light
17. _____ Solstice is when we have the shortest amount of daylight for that year and the longest night

Down

1. The coming apart of an atom that gives off a lot of energy
2. The coming together of 2 atoms that releases a lot of energy - more than fission!
5. smallest planet- slowest rotation- magnetic
6. most like earth size wise- atmospheric pressure able to crush us- retrograde rotation
8. Fastest rotation (a little less than half an earth day)- largest planet- 29 years for 1 trip around the Sun- known also for Great Red Spot
11. Last planet in our solar system- Dark blue and windy-
12. Dwarf planet found just inside the Kuiper Belt- has a few moons- orbit actually crosses Neptune periodically
15. _____ Equinox is an occurrence in the fall where the daylight and nighttime are equivalent
17. the amount of moon that you can see is increasing
18. the amount of moon that you can see is decreasing
19. During a _____ Eclipse the shadow of the earth goes across the face of the moon

9th Grade Science: Organelles

Organelles are the inside elements of a cell that are responsible for all of the tasks that keep the cell healthy and alive. Each organelle has a distinct function. The word "organelle" means "small organ," and these tiny powerhouses are responsible for everything from defending the cell to repairing/healing, assisting in the development, removing waste products, and even reproduction. The function of each organelle is also influenced by the functions of other organelles. The cell will perish if any organelle fails to perform its function.

Many of the same types of organelles exist in both plant and animal cells, and they function in similar ways. Both plant and animal cells have a total of ten organelles.

Plant-like cells, on the other hand, are built solely for photosynthesis and utilize the rigid wall, as well as organelles that operate to generate energy from sunlight. Organelles in animal-like cells have a lot greater variety and capability.

Match each term with a definition.

1	F	nucleus	→	where DNA is stored
2	J	lysosomes	→	degradation of proteins and cellular waste
3	G	Golgi Apparatus	→	modification of proteins; "post-office" of the cell
4	A	Mitochondria	→	powerhouse of the cell
5	B	SER	→	lipid synthesis
6	C	RER	→	protein synthesis + modifications
7	E	Microtubules	→	responsible for chromosome segregation
8	D	ribosomes	→	protein synthesis
9	K	peroxysomes	→	degradation of H_2O_2
10	I	cell wall	→	prevents excessive uptake of water, protects the cell (in plants)
11	L	chloroplast	→	site of photosynthesis
12	H	central vacuole	→	stores water in plant cells

Shakespeare: Romeo and Juliet

Across

1. an enemy or opponent
2. something surrendered or subject to surrender as punishment for a crime, an offense, an error, or a breach of contract
3. loathsome; disgusting
7. to expel or banish a person from his or her country
8. to feel sorry for; regret
12. a small container, as of glass, for holding liquids
15. long and tiresome

Down

3. boldly courageous; brave; stout-hearted
5. to express disapproval of; scold; reproach
6. a musician, singer, or poet
9. an expression of grief or sorrow
10. to flood or to overwhelm
11. a malicious, false, or defamatory statement or report
13. infliction of injury, harm, humiliation, or the like, on a person by another who has been harmed by that person; violent revenge
14. to read through with thoroughness or care

VALIANT   LAMENT   SLANDER
MINSTREL   PERUSE
TEDIOUS   CHIDE   EXILE
VILE   FORFEIT   INUNDATE
REPENT   ADVERSARY   VIAL
VENGEANCE

Match Elements of the Periodic Table

The periodic table is the most important source of chemistry information. It arranges all of the known elements in a useful array. Elements are arranged in increasing atomic number order from left to right and top to bottom. The periodic table lists all known elements, grouping those with similar properties together.

A substance that cannot be broken down into another substance is referred to as an element. There are approximately 100 elements, each with its own atom type. Atoms of at least one or more elements can be found in everything in the universe. The periodic table lists all known elements, grouping those with similar properties together.

Match the chemical element in the first column with the correct abbreviation from the second column. Write the corresponding letter for each element in the box.

1	E		Dubnium	→	Db
2	H		Seaborgium	→	Sg
3	F		Bohrium	→	Bh
4	G		Hassium	→	Hs
5	N		Meitnerium	→	Mt
6	J		Darmstadtium	→	Ds
7	A		Roentgenium	→	Rg
8	B		Copernicium	→	Cn
9	K		Nihonium	→	Nh
10	I		Flerovium	→	Fl
11	D		Moscovium	→	Mc
12	M		Livermorium	→	Lv
13	C		Tennessine	→	Ts
14	L		Oganesson	→	Og

9th Grade HEALTH: Foods and Nutrition

Nutrition aids in the maintenance of a healthy immune system. Because our immune system is our first line of defense against diseases, poor nutrition can make us more susceptible to them.

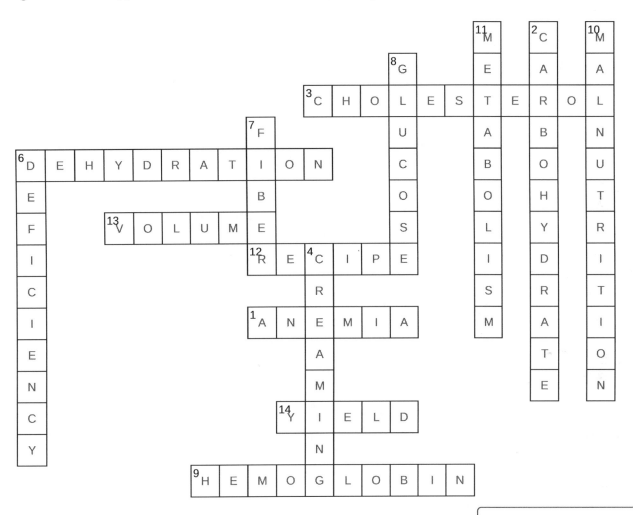

Across

1. blood disorder caused by lack of iron
3. fat-like substance in cells needed for many body processes
6. a condition in which the body has too little water
9. a protein that transports oxygen in the blood
12. a set of directions for making a food or beverage
13. the amount of space an ingredient takes up
14. the amount or number of servings a recipe makes

Down

2. essential nutrient that is the body's main source of energy
4. in baking, blending fat and sugar thoroughly together before adding other ingredients
6. too little of an essential nutrient
7. the parts of fruits, vegetables, grains and legumes that cannot be digested
8. blood sugar, the body's basic fuel
10. poor nourishment resulting from a lack of nutrients
11. the rate at which the body uses nutrients to provide energy

VOLUME   CHOLESTEROL
ANEMIA   RECIPE
DEHYDRATION
DEFICIENCY   GLUCOSE
CREAMING   YIELD
METABOLISM
HEMOGLOBIN
MALNUTRITION   FIBER
CARBOHYDRATE

9th Grade Health: Immune System

white	defends	cell-mediated	cells	Immune
external	Macrophages	signals	foreign	invading

Your immune system __defends__ you against harmful intruders. __Immune__ responses occur when your body's immune system detects threats. Learn about antibody-mediated and cell-mediated immunity.

Your immune system, which detects and eliminates __foreign__ invaders, provides this tremendous service. An immunological reaction occurs when your body's immune system detects __external__ intruders. Your immune system is a great asset that selflessly protects you from antigens, or foreign intruders.

Immunity by Cells

Antibody-mediated immunity is one of your immune system's two arms. The other arm is __cell-mediated__ immunity, which helps the body get rid of undesired cells like infected, cancerous, or transplanted cells. __Macrophages__ consume antigens in this sort of immunity. If you split down macrophages, you can remember it easily. Big indicates macro- and phages means 'eaters.' So macrophages are voracious consumers of antigens. The macrophage then chews up the antigen and displays the fragments on its surface.

When helper T cells encounter macrophages, they give out __signals__ that activate other __white__ blood __cells__ , such as cytotoxic or killer T cells. These killer T cells multiply fast, forming an army ready to battle and eliminate the __invading__ cell that prompted the immune response.

9th Grade Grammar:
Contractions Multiple Choice

Simply put, you replace the letter(s) that were removed from the original words with an apostrophe when you make the contraction.

1. Here is
   a. Here's
   b. Heres'

2. One is
   a. Ones'
   b. One's

3. I will
   a. Il'l
   b. I'll

4. You will
   a. You'll
   b. Yo'ill

5. She will
   a. She'll
   b. She'ill

6. He will
   a. He'ill
   b. He'll

7. It will
   a. It'ill
   b. It'll

8. We will
   a. We'll
   b. We'ill

9. They will
   a. They'ill
   b. They'll

10. That will
   a. That'l
   b. That'll

11. There will
   a. There'ill
   b. There'll

12. This will
   a. This'll
   b. This'ill

13. What will
   a. What'ill
   b. What'll

14. Who will
   a. Who'll
   b. Whol'l

9th Grade History: Henry VIII

1. True
2. False
3. False
4. True
5. False
6. True
7. True
8. False
9. True
10. True
11. False
12. True
13. True
14. False
15. True
16. False
17. False
18. True
19. False
20. True
21. True
22. False
23. True
24. True
25. True
26. False
27. False
28. False
29. True
30. True

Languages & Nationalities

1. Albanian

   a. albanés

   b. noruego

3. Bosnian

   a. bosnio

   b. árabe

5. Czech

   a. portugués

   b. checo

7. Dutch

   a. holandés

   b. ucraniano

9. Hungarian

   a. húngaro

   b. irlandés

11. Norwegian

   a. noruego

   b. esloveno

13. Portuguese

   a. danés

   b. portugués

15. Slovenian

   a. esloveno

   b. bosnio

17. Turkish

   a. turco

   b. albanés

2. Arabian

   a. árabe

   b. rumano

4. Bulgarian

   a. portugués

   b. búlgaro

6. Danish

   a. noruego

   b. danés

8. Hebrew

   a. hebreo

   b. húngaro

10. Irish

   a. árabe

   b. irlandés

12. Polish

   a. sueco

   b. polaco

14. Romanian

   a. rumano

   b. checo

16. Swedish

   a. albanés

   b. sueco

18. Ukrainian

   a. rumano

   b. ucraniano

9th Grade Geography: Landform

A landform is a natural or man-made feature of the Earth's or another planet's solid surface. A given terrain is made up of landforms, and their arrangement in the landscape is known as topography.

1. Lakes are an inland body of water, usually fresh
   - a. True
   - b. False

2. A sea is the direction from which a river flows
   - a. True
   - b. False

3. A delta is the land deposited at the mouth of a river
   - a. True
   - b. False

4. What landform is surrounded by water on three sides?
   - a. An island
   - b. A peninsula

5. A river is a narrow man-made channel of water that joins other bodies of water
   - a. True
   - b. False

6. The mouth is where a river flows into a larger body of water.
   - a. True
   - b. False

7. Which of the following is NOT a landform?
   - a. An island
   - b. A river

8. Downstream is the direction toward which a river flows.
   - a. True
   - b. False

9. A sea is a large area of salt water smaller than an ocean.
   - a. True
   - b. False

10. A bay is land deposited at the mouth of a river.
    - a. True
    - b. False

11. How are a valley and a canyon alike?
    - a. They are both tall landforms.
    - b. They are both low landforms.

12. A canal is a man-made channel of water that joins other bodies of water.
    - a. True
    - b. False

13. A lake is a place where a river begins.
    - a. True
    - b. False

14. Which types of landforms are always flat?
    - a. Plateaus and plains
    - b. Hills and peninsulas

9th Grade Geography: Know Your World

Test your knowledge of global, national, and local geography, as well as the environment.

1. Spain can be found in which continent
   a. Europe
   b. New Zealand
   c. Bogota

2. Uganda can be found in which continent
   a. Canberra
   b. Africa
   c. Lake Taupo

3. Uruguay can be found in which continent
   a. South America
   b. Atlantic Ocean
   c. Bogota

4. Beijing is the capital city of
   a. China
   b. Samoa
   c. New York

5. Honshu is an island of what country
   a. Japan
   b. Suva
   c. New York

6. Apia is the capital city of
   a. Bogota
   b. Samoa
   c. Brasilia

7. The Amazon River can be found in which continent
   a. Suva
   b. Buenos Aires
   c. South America

8. The Southern Alps can be found in which country
   a. Portugal
   b. New Zealand
   c. Brasilia

9. The Andes Mountains can be found in which continent
   a. Brasilia
   b. South America
   c. Berlin

10. Lines of longitude run
   a. Vertical - North to South
   b. Wellington
   c. Samoa

11. Lines of latitude run
   a. Horizontal - East to West
   b. Suva
   c. Italy

12. The ocean between the Americas and Europe and Africa is the
   a. Africa
   b. Italy
   c. Atlantic Ocean

13. The capital city of France is
   a. Bogota
   b. Paris
   c. Buenos Aires

14. The capital city of Germany is
   a. Berlin
   b. New Zealand
   c. Moscow

15. The capital city of Russia is
   a. Moscow
   b. Buenos Aires
   c. Paris

16. The capital city of the United States is
   a. Brasilia
   b. Washington D.C
   c. China

17. The capital city of Fiji is
   a. Suva
   b. Portugal
   c. Buenos Aires

18. Mt Everest can be found in what continent
   a. Asia
   b. Japan
   c. Wellington

19. Switzerland is a country in
   a. Europe
   b. Wellington
   c. Portugal

20. The capital city of Brazil is
   a. Japan
   b. China
   c. Brasilia

21. The capital city of Colombia is
   a. Spain
   b. Bogota
   c. Japan

22. The capital city of Argentina is
   a. Buenos Aires
   b. Portugal
   c. Bogota

23. Vietnam can be found in what continent
   a. Asia
   b. Berlin
   c. Vertical - North to South

24. Libya can be found in what continent
   a. Africa
   b. Bogota
   c. New York

25. Rome is the capital city of which European country
   a. Buenos Aires
   b. Italy
   c. Paris

26. Madrid is the capital city of which European country
   a. Brasilia
   b. Europe
   c. Spain

27. Lisbon is the capital city of which European country
   a. Samoa
   b. Portugal
   c. Buenos Aires

28. The Statue of Liberty can be found in what US city
   a. Italy
   b. New York
   c. Paris

29. The capital city of New Zealand is
   a. Canberra
   b. Wellington
   c. Washington D.C

30. The capital city of Australia is
   a. China
   b. Moscow
   c. Canberra

9th Grade Art: Roman Portrait Sculptures

Alexander	aristocrats	ancestral	shrine	rewarded
sculpture	pattern	mosaics	marble	artistic

Portrait __sculpture__ has been practiced since the beginning of Roman history. It was most likely influenced by the Roman practice of creating __ancestral__ images. When a Roman man died, his family made a wax sculpture of his face and kept it in a special __shrine__ at home. Because these sculptures were more like records of a person's life than works of art, the emphasis was on realistic detail rather than __artistic__ beauty.

As Rome became more prosperous and gained access to Greek sculptors, Roman __aristocrats__ known as patricians began creating these portraits from stone rather than wax.

Roman sculpture was about more than just honoring the dead; it was also about honoring the living. Important Romans were __rewarded__ for their valor or greatness by having statues of themselves erected and displayed in public. This is one of the earliest of these types of statues that we've discovered, and the __pattern__ continued all the way until the Republic's demise.

The mosaic is the only form of Roman art that has yet to be discussed. The Romans adored mosaics and created them with exquisite skill. The Romans created __mosaics__ of unprecedented quality and detail using cubes of naturally colored __marble__ . The floor mosaic depicting __Alexander__ the Great at the Battle of Issus is probably the most famous Roman mosaic.

9th Grade Art: Pop Art

In 1957, Richard Hamilton described the style, writing: "Pop art is: **popular, transient, expendable, low-cost, mass-produced, young, witty, sexy, gimmicky, glamorous and big business**."

humor	events	spread	founded	activists
Gallery	artists	pioneer	vibrant	celebrity

Pop art was __founded__ in the mid-1950s in Britain by the Independent Group, a group of painters, sculptors, writers, and critics. It quickly spread to the United States. Much of the movement's origins can be traced back to a cultural revolution led by __activists__, thinkers, and __artists__ who sought to restructure a conformist social order. Many believe that U.K. Pop __pioneer__ Richard Hamilton's 1956 collage is responsible for the movement's rapid __spread__. Just what is it that makes today's homes so different, so appealing? Its appearance in London's Whitechapel __Gallery__ marked the official start of the cultural phenomenon.

Images and icons from popular media and products were used in pop art. This included commercial items such as soup cans, road signs, __celebrity__ photos, newspapers, and other items common in the commercial world. Brand names and logos were also used.

Pop art is distinguished by its use of __vibrant__, bright colors. The primary colors red, yellow, and blue were prominent pigments in many well-known works, particularly in Roy Lichtenstein's body of work.

One of the most important aspects of Pop art was __humor__. Artists use the subject matter to make a point about current __events__, mock fads, and question the status quo.

1. George Washington was born on _____.
   a. 02-22-1732
   b. February 24, 1732

2. The United States Constitution is the law of the ____.
   a. land
   b. world

3. George's _____ had deteriorated.
   a. teeth
   b. feet

4. George Washington can be seen on a _____.
   a. one-dollar bill
   b. five-dollar bill

5. George's father died when he was 20 years old.
   a. True
   b. False

6. George was a plantation owner.
   a. True
   b. False

7. George married the widow _____.
   a. Martha Custis
   b. Mary Curtis

8. In his will, Washington freed his _____.
   a. children
   b. slaves

9. George served in the _____ legislature.
   a. Virginia
   b. Maryland

10. George Washington was elected as the _____ President of the USA.
    a. forth
    b. first

11. A widow is someone whose husband has died.
    a. True
    b. False

12. George died on December 14, 1699.
    a. True
    b. False

13. George grew up in _____.
    a. Washington DC
    b. Colonial Virginia

14. The capital of the United States is named after George.
    a. True
    b. False

15. A plantation is a town that is tended by a large number of officials.
    a. True
    b. False

16. Washington caught a _____ just a few years after leaving the presidency.
    a. cold
    b. flight

1. Hanson served from November 5, 1781 until December 3, 1782
   a. True
   b. False

2. Hanson really LOVED his job.
   a. True
   b. False

3. Under the Articles of Confederation, the United States had no _____.
   a. executive branch
   b. congress office

4. The President of Congress was a _____ position within the Confederation Congress.
   a. senate
   b. ceremonial

5. In November 1781, Hanson became the first President of the United States in Congress Assembled, under the _____.
   a. Articles of Congress
   b. Articles of Confederation

6. _____ men were appointed to serve one year terms as president under the Articles of Confederation.
   a. Eight
   b. Two

7. Hanson was able to remove all _____ troops from American lands.
   a. foreign
   b. USA

8. Hanson is also responsible for establishing _____ as the fourth Thursday in November.
   a. Christmas Day
   b. Thanksgiving Day

9. Instead of the four year term that current Presidents serve, Presidents under the Articles of Confederation served only ___ year.
   a. one
   b. three

10. Hanson died on November 15, 1783 at the age of _____.
    a. 64
    b. sixty-two

11. Both George Washington and Hanson are commemorated with _____ in the United States Capitol in Washington, D.C.
    a. houses
    b. statues

12. George Washington in the military sphere and John Hanson in the _____ sphere.
    a. presidential
    b. political

9th Grade Biology: Heredity

1.

a. Chromosomes

2.

a. Proteins

3.

a. True

4.

a. Polydactyl cats.

5.

a. Humans creating offspring through sexual reproduction.

6.

a. Parent.

7.

a. True

8.

a. A chart that shows chromosome pairs.

9.

a. Identical

10.

a. Fragmentation

11.

a. Binary fission

12.

a. Fragmentation

13.

a. Regeneration

14.

a. Parthenogenesis

15.

a. True

16.

a. False

17.

a. Physical

18.

a. Deoxyribonucleic Acid

19.

a. True

20.

a. 25%

ADDITIONAL ASSIGNMENTS PLANNER

○ MONDAY

GOALS THIS WEEK

_____

_____

_____

○ TUESDAY

_____

_____

_____

○ WEDNESDAY

WHAT TO STUDY

_____

_____

○ THURSDAY

_____

_____

_____

_____

○ FRIDAY

_____

_____

_____

_____

EXTRA CREDIT WEEKEND WORK
○ SATURDAY / SUNDAY

_____

_____

_____

_____

ADDITIONAL ASSIGNMENTS PLANNER

○ MONDAY

○ TUESDAY

○ WEDNESDAY

○ THURSDAY

○ FRIDAY

EXTRA CREDIT WEEKEND WORK
○ SATURDAY / SUNDAY

GOALS THIS WEEK

WHAT TO STUDY

ADDITIONAL ASSIGNMENTS PLANNER

○ MONDAY

GOALS THIS WEEK

_____

_____

○ TUESDAY

_____

_____

_____

○ WEDNESDAY

_____

WHAT TO STUDY

_____

_____

○ THURSDAY

_____

_____

_____

○ FRIDAY

_____

_____

_____

_____

EXTRA CREDIT WEEKEND WORK
○ SATURDAY / SUNDAY

_____

_____

ADDITIONAL ASSIGNMENTS PLANNER

○ MONDAY

GOALS THIS WEEK

_____

_____

_____

○ TUESDAY

_____

_____

_____

_____

○ WEDNESDAY

WHAT TO STUDY

_____

_____

○ THURSDAY

_____

_____

_____

_____

○ FRIDAY

_____

_____

_____

_____

EXTRA CREDIT WEEKEND WORK
○ SATURDAY / SUNDAY

_____

_____

_____

_____

GRADES TRACKER

Week	Monday	Tuesday	Wednesday	Thursday	Friday
1					
2					
3					
4					
5					
6					
7					
8					
9					
10					
11					
12					
13					
14					
15					
16					
17					
18					

Notes

GRADES TRACKER

Week	Monday	Tuesday	Wednesday	Thursday	Friday
1					
2					
3					
4					
5					
6					
7					
8					
9					
10					
11					
12					
13					
14					
15					
16					
17					
18					

Notes

End of the Year Evaluation

Name: _____

Grade/Level: _____ Date: _____

Subjects Studied: _____
_____
_____

Goals Accomplished: _____
_____
_____
_____

Most Improved Areas: _____
_____
_____
_____

Areas of Improvement: _____
_____
_____

Main Curriculum Evaluation	Satisfied		A= Above Standards	Final Grades
_____	Yes	No	S= Meets Standards	
			N= Needs Improvement	_____
_____	Yes	No	98-100 A+	
			93-97 A	_____
_____	Yes	No	90-92 A	
			88-89 B+	_____
_____	Yes	No	83-87 B	
			80-82 B	_____
_____	Yes	No	78-79 C+	
			73-77 C	_____
			70-72 C	
_____	Yes	No	68-69 D+	_____
			62-67 D	
			60-62 D	
			59 & Below F	

Most Enjoyed: _____
_____

Least Enjoyed: _____
_____

Made in the USA
Las Vegas, NV
22 June 2024

91349573R00065